GW01158469

Questions and Answers

Q&A

SCIENCE
Single and Double Awards
KEY STAGE 4

Bob McDuell & Graham Booth

Chief Examiners

SERIES EDITOR: BOB McDUELL

Letts
EDUCATIONAL

Contents

HOW TO USE THIS BOOK

The aim of the *Questions and Answers* series is to provide you with help to do as well as possible in your exams at GCSE or, in Scotland, at General and Credit levels. This book is based on the idea that an experienced Examiner can give, through examination questions, sample answers and advice, the help students need to secure success and improve their grades.

The *Questions and Answers* series is designed to provide the following:

- **Introductory advice** on the different types of question and how to answer them to maximise your marks.
- Information about other skills, apart from the recall of knowledge, that will be tested on examination papers. These are sometimes called **Assessment objectives** and include communication, problem solving, evaluation and interpretation (see pages 4–5). The *Questions and Answers* series is intended to develop these skills by showing you how marks are allocated.
- **Revision summaries** to remind you of the topics you will need to have revised in order to answer examination questions.
- Many examples of **examination questions**, arranged by topic, with spaces for you to fill in your answers, just as on an examination paper. Only try the questions once you have revised a topic thoroughly. Read the Revision summary, before attempting the questions, to double-check you know the topic. It is best not to consult the answers before trying the questions.
- **Sample answers** to all of the questions.
- **Advice from Examiners**. By using the experience of actual Chief Examiners we are able to give advice on how you can improve your answers and avoid the most common mistakes.

THE IMPORTANCE OF USING QUESTIONS FOR REVISION

Past examination questions play an important part in revising for examinations. However, it is important not to start practising questions too early. Nothing can be more disheartening than trying to do a question which you do not understand because you have not mastered the topic. Therefore, it is important to have studied a topic thoroughly before attempting any questions on it.

How can past examination questions provide a way of preparing for the examination? It is unlikely that any question you try will appear in exactly the same form on the papers you are going to take. However, the examiner is restricted on what can be set because the questions must cover the whole syllabus and test certain Assessment objectives. The number of totally original questions that can be set on any part of the syllabus is very limited and so similar ideas occur over and over again. It certainly will help you if the question you are trying to answer in an examination is familiar and you know that you have done similar questions before. This is a great boost for your confidence and confidence is what is required for examination success.

Practising examination questions will also highlight gaps in your knowledge and understanding which you can go back and revise more thoroughly. It will also indicate which sorts of questions you can do well and which, if there is a choice of questions, you should avoid.

Attempting past questions will get you used to the type of language used in questions.

Finally, having access to answers, as you do in this book, will enable you to see clearly what is required by the examiner, how best to answer each question, and the amount of detail required. Attention to detail is a key aspect of achieving success at GCSE.

EXAMINATION TECHNIQUE

Success in GCSE examinations comes from proper preparation and a positive attitude to the examination. This book is intended to help you overcome 'examination nerves' which often come from a fear of not being properly prepared. Examination technique is extremely important and certainly affects your performance. Remember the basics:

- read the questions carefully;
- make sure that you watch the time carefully and complete the paper; it is no good answering one question well if you spend so long doing it that you do not answer another question at all;
- read the rubric on the front of the examination paper carefully to make sure you know how many questions to attempt;
- examination papers usually tell you how many marks are available for each answer; take notice of this information as the number of marks gives a guide to the importance of the question and often to the amount which you ought to write;
- check before the end of the examination that you have not missed any pages and remember to turn over the last page;
- remember to leave time to check through your work carefully.

TYPES OF EXAMINATION QUESTION

Which tier should you enter?

GCSE Science papers in England and Wales are set in two tiers – Foundation and Higher. There are only certain grades available for each tier. It is important you enter the correct tier.

Foundation	Higher
	A*
	A
	B
C	C
D	D
E	
F	
G	
U	

You can be awarded a C or D grade on either tier. If you are aiming at a grade above C you need to take the Higher tier. If you are working at D or even C, you are probably better advised to take the Foundation tier, because if you fail to achieve a grade D on Higher tier you will be ungraded.

Approximately 45% of the marks will be for common questions set on both Higher and Foundation papers. They will be the easy questions on the Higher tier paper and the hard questions on the Foundation tier paper. These questions are used by the Examiners to ensure that grades C and D on the two papers are equivalent. If we assume that each paper contains approximately 20% of the marks for each available grade, a Higher tier paper will have a lot of questions which C grade candidates cannot hope to do, so the mark required for a grade C on Foundation and Higher will be very different.

The questions used on GCSE papers are Short Answer and Structured Questions of varying lengths. Most of the questions in this book are of this type. The reason they are used so widely is because they are so versatile. They can be short, with little opportunity for extended writing but giving good syllabus coverage. This makes them very suitable for questions testing lower grades on

Foundation tier papers. Alternatively, they can be longer and more complex in their structure, with opportunities for extended writing and the demonstration of higher levels of interpretation and evaluation. In this form they are very suitable for questions targeted at A* and A grades on Higher tier papers.

In a structured question, the question is divided into parts (a), (b), (c), etc. These parts can be further subdivided into (i), (ii), (iii), (iv), etc. A structure is built into the question and hence into your answer. This is where the term structured question comes from.

For each part of the question there are a number of lines or a space for your answer. This is a guide to you about the detail required in the answer, but it does not have to limit you. If you require more space continue your answer on a separate sheet of paper, but make sure you label the answer clearly, e.g. 3(a)(ii).

For each part of the question there is a number in brackets, e.g. (3), to show you how many marks are allocated to this part of the question by the examiner. If a part is worth three marks, for example, the question requires more than one or two words. As a general rule, if there are three marks allocated, you will need to make three points. To give you a guide as you work through structured questions, papers are often designed to enable you to score one mark per minute. A question worth a maximum of fifteen marks should therefore take about fifteen minutes to answer.

You do not have to write your answers in full sentences. Concise notes are often the most suitable response. Read your answers to yourself, not aloud, and check that they make sense.

It is most important to read the stimulus material in the question thoroughly and more than once. This information is often not used fully by students and, as a result, the question is not answered fully. The key to answering many of these questions comes from the appreciation of the full meaning of the 'command word' at the start of the question – 'state', 'describe', 'explain'.

The following glossary of command words may help you in the answering of structured questions.

- **State** This means a brief answer is required, with no supporting evidence. Alternatives include **write down**, **give**, **list**, **name**.
- **Define** Just a definition is required.
- **State and explain** A short answer is required (see **state**) but then an explanation is required. A question of this type should be worth more than one mark.
- **Describe** This is often used with reference to a particular experiment. The important points should be given about each stage. Again this type of question is worth more than one mark.
- **Outline** The answer should be brief and the main points picked out.
- **Predict** A brief answer is required, without supporting evidence. You are required to make logical links between various pieces of information.
- **Complete** You are required to add information to a diagram, sentence, flow chart, graph, key, table, etc.
- **Find** This is a general term which may mean calculate, measure, determine, etc.
- **Calculate** A numerical answer is required. You should show your working in order to get an answer. Do not forget the correct units.
- **Suggest** There is not just one correct answer or you are applying your answer to a situation outside the syllabus.

ASSESSMENT OBJECTIVES IN SCIENCE

Assessment Objectives are the intellectual and practical skills you should be able to show. Opportunities must be made by the Examiner when setting the examination paper for you to demonstrate your mastery of these skills when you answer the question paper.

Traditionally, the Assessment objective of knowledge and understanding has been regarded as the most important skill to develop. Candidates have been directed to learn large bodies of knowledge to recall in the examination. Whilst not wanting in any way to devalue the learning of facts, it should be remembered that on modern papers knowledge and understanding can only contribute about half of the marks available. The other half of the marks are acquired by mastery of the other Assessment objectives. namely to:

- communicate scientific observations, ideas and arguments effectively;
- select and use reference materials and translate data from one form to another;
- interpret, evaluate and make informed judgements from relevant facts, observations and phenomena;
- solve qualitative and quantitative problems.

1 Communicate scientific observations, ideas and arguments effectively
(*weighting on papers approximately 5–10%*)

In any examination, communication of information to the examiner is of primary importance. Questions are built into the paper to test your ability to communicate scientific information. Often these questions require extended answers. In this type of question it is important to look at your answer objectively after you have written it and try to judge whether your answer is communicating information effectively.

2 Select and use reference materials and translate data from one form to another (*weighting on papers approximately 10–15%*)

In questions testing this Assessment objective you are frequently asked to pick information from a chart or table and use it in another form, e.g. to draw a graph, a pie chart, bar chart, etc. You may be asked to complete a table using information from a graph.

It is important to transfer the skills you have acquired in mathematics to your work in science.

Skill acquired	Approx. grade in GCSE maths
Read information from graphs or simple diagrams	F
Work out simple percentages	F
Construct and use pie charts	F
Use graphs	E
Plot graphs from data provided. The axes and scales are given to you	E
Able to draw line of best fit through points on a graph	C
Select the most appropriate axes and scales for graph plotting	B

It is reasonable, therefore, to conclude that at Higher tier you might be required to use a blank piece of graph paper and choose your own scales and axes. Then you would plot the points and draw a line of best fit through the points. If you are doing this, remember the following:

❶ Draw your graph as large as possible on the graph paper by choosing scales appropriately. Avoid choosing scales where, for example, 3 small squares are equivalent to 5°C. It would be better if 1 small square was equivalent to 1°C or 2°C. With this type of graph drawing, marks are usually awarded for the choice of scales and for labelled axes.

❷ Plot each point with a dot or small cross. Circle the dot or cross to make its position clear.

❸ Your line of best fit, whether it is a straight line or a curve, does not have to go through all the points. Some points may not be in the correct place, even if you plotted them correctly, because of inaccuracies in the experiment or experimental error.

On a Foundation tier paper a similar graph may have to be drawn, but it would be more appropriate for the Examiner to give you a grid with axes and scales given. Then you would only have to plot the points and draw the line of best fit. It would probably be worth fewer marks than a graph on the Higher tier paper.

3 Interpret, evaluate and make informed judgements from relevant facts, observations and phenomena (*weighting on papers approximately 10–15%*)

Questions testing this Assessment Objective are often difficult for candidates. It is much easier to test this on a Higher tier paper than on a Foundation tier paper.

The command word 'suggest' is very frequently used, as the information given, perhaps in a paragraph, table, diagram or any combination of these, and is open to more than one interpretation.

Look carefully at all of the information given and look for possible alternative interpretations before writing your answer.

4 Solve qualitative and quantitative problems (*weighting on papers approximately 10–15%*)

There is no shortage of opportunities to ask questions testing this Assessment objective on science GCSE papers. Again opportunities are greater, especially for solving quantitative problems, on Higher tier papers.

Qualitative problems can include writing equations and the use of qualitative tests, for example, to distinguish sulphuric and hydrochloric acids.

Quantitative problems include the full range of calculations. Remember, when attempting to carry out a calculation, to:

❶ Recall the correct formula. There is usually a mark for being able to recall the formula. The formulae you are required to know are given on p.6.

Remember if you cannot recall the formula you will be unable to score marks on other parts of the question which require you to use the formula.

❷ Use all of the information given to you. If the question gives relative atomic masses, they should be used.

❸ Show all of your working, so credit can be given if you do not get the correct answer but get some way through the question.

❹ Take care when substituting in a mathematical formula to be consistent in your units.

❺ Give correct units to your answers if there are units. Remember ratios, including relative atomic masses and relative densities, do not have units.

Throughout this book you will see questions where the question is designed to test Assessment objectives other than knowledge and understanding.

Formulae that you should know

This is a list of formulae that you may need to use in answering physics questions but will not be given to you either on the examination paper or on a separate formula sheet.

For Foundation tier papers

power = current × voltage $P = I \times V$

voltage = current × resistance $V = I \times R$

average speed = distance travelled ÷ time taken $v = \dfrac{s}{t}$

acceleration = increase in velocity ÷ time taken $a = \dfrac{(v\text{-}u)}{t}$

pressure = force ÷ area $P = \dfrac{F}{A}$

work done or energy transfer = force × distance moved in its own direction
$$W = F \times d$$

In addition, for Higher tier papers

charge = current × time $Q = I \times t$

$\dfrac{\text{primary voltage}}{\text{secondary voltage}} = \dfrac{\text{number of primary turns}}{\text{number of secondary turns}}$ $\dfrac{V_p}{V_s} = \dfrac{N_p}{N_s}$

force = mass × acceleration $F = m \times a$

wave speed = frequency × wavelength $v = f \times \lambda$

Any other formulae that you need will be provided on the examination paper or on a separate formula sheet

All living things have seven life processes in common:

● they all **grow**

● they all **respire**; respiration is the process that takes place in all cells that involves the release of energy from food

● they are all **sensitive**; this means that they respond to changes in their environment, for example changes in light level

● they all **move**; even plants that have roots move as they grow

● they all **excrete**; they get rid of waste by-products

● they all **feed**; plants make their own food that they then use in the process of respiration

● they all **reproduce**; reproduction is essential for survival of the species

All plants and animals are made up of cells. Some simple plants and animals have only one cell or a small number of cells that have to carry out all the life processes. In more complex plants and animals individual cells have specific jobs to do. The diagram shows typical plant and animal cells.

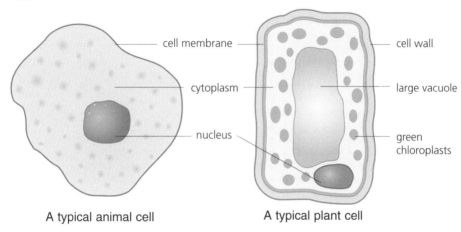

cell membrane — cytoplasm — nucleus

cell wall — large vacuole — green chloroplasts

A typical animal cell

A typical plant cell

Plant cells have a cell wall to help to give them rigidity. All types of cell need to allow substances to pass into them so that, for example, respiration can take place. They also need to allow the waste products of respiration to pass out of them. The cell membrane is partially permeable, which means that it only allows certain particles to pass through it. There are three mechanisms by which substances pass into and out of a cell; **diffusion**, **osmosis** and **active transport**.

Diffusion describes the spreading out of particles from areas of high concentration to areas of low concentration. An example of diffusion is the movement of oxygen from air sacs into blood capillaries in the alveoli; carbon dioxide diffuses in the opposite direction.

Osmosis is a type of diffusion; it refers to the movement of water through a partially-permeable membrane. If there is a difference in the water concentration at each side of the membrane then water moves from the region of higher water concentration to the region of lower water concentration until the concentrations are equal. Water moves through living cells by osmosis.

Movement of substances from an area of low concentration to an area of high concentration is necessary for root hairs to absorb minerals from the soil. Movement against the natural flow caused by diffusion is called active transport; it needs an energy supply to drive it.

The nucleus of a cell contains all the information that an organism needs to be able to carry out the life processes. Each piece of information is in the form of a gene, and many genes together make up a chromosome.

As organisms grow, new cells are continually being made by a process called **mitosis**. In mitosis, the chromosomes first duplicate themselves and then the cell divides into two, so that each new cell has an exact copy of the chromosomes of the original cell.

The diagram below summarises mitosis.

Simple cell – nucleus contains 2 pairs of chromosomes

   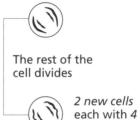

The rest of the
cell divides

2 new cells
each with *4*
chromosomes

2 pairs of
chromosomes   They double   and separate into
two groups

When an organism reproduces sexually, a single cell is formed by the fusion of two gametes (sex cells). In order that the new cell has the correct number of chromosomes, each gamete must have half the number of a normal cell. In humans, most cells have 46 chromosomes, arranged in 23 pairs. When fertilisation takes place, an egg and a sperm each with 23 chromosomes fuse together to form a single cell that has 46 chromosomes.

Gametes are produced by a form of cell division called **meiosis**, which results in each gamete having half the number of normal cells. In meiosis, after the chromosomes have copied, the cell divides into four new cells, so each cell has half the number of chromosomes of the original cell.

The diagram summarises meiosis.

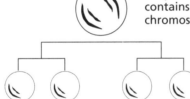

Simple cell – nucleus
contains 2 pairs of
chromosomes

4 new cells, each with only *2*
chromosomes (gametes: formed
in the sex cells of males and
females)

**If you need to
revise this
subject more
thoroughly,
see the relevant
topics in the
Letts GCSE
*Science
Study Guide* or
CD-ROM.**

In animals, large numbers of similar cells make up tissues. Muscular tissue can contract and cause movement; glandular tissue can make useful substances and xylem tissue can transport water. Groups of tissues in turn form organ systems, each system being adapted to do a particular job.

The main organ systems in humans are the reproductive system, the digestive system, the circulatory system, the gas exchange system, the nervous system, the endocrine system and the excretory system.

1 (a) The table below shows named human cells and plant cells. Complete the table to explain
   how each labelled part helps the cell with an important function. The first one has been
   done for you.   (5)

Name of cell	Diagram of cell	How the labelled part helps the cell
Red blood cell	large area of cell membrane	*Allows the cell to take in more oxygen.*
Sperm	long tail	
Ovum (egg cell)	large amount of cytoplasm	
Neurone (nerve cell)	long nerve fibre	
Leaf (palisade) cell	many chloroplasts	
Root hair cell	large area of cell membrane	

(b) All the cells in the table, other than the red blood cells, have TWO parts in common.
   Name them.

   1 ....

   2 .... (2)

(c) Some human cells contain 46 chromosomes, some contain 23 chromosomes and some contain no chromosomes.

Complete the table below by writing in the number of chromosomes in each named human cell. You may use each number once, more than once or not at all. The first one has been done for you. (4)

Human cell	Number of chromosomes
Muscle cell	46
Sperm	
Ovum (egg cell)	
Neurone (nerve cell)	
Red blood cell (mature)	

Edexcel 1996

2 There are seven life processes common to all living things.

(a) Name the process by which:

(i) organisms get rid of waste products ....

(ii) new organisms are produced ....

(iii) energy is released from food .... (3)

(b) All organisms form new cells by cell division. Two ways in which this occurs are mitosis and meiosis.

(i) Use diagrams to describe what happens when cells divide by mitosis. (3)

(ii) Write down two differences in the outcome of cell division by meiosis compared to cell division by mitosis.

1 ....

2 .... (2)

3 The data in the table represents uptake of sulphate ions by barley plants under three different conditions. The plants were given sulphate labelled with a radioactive isotope of sulphur (^{35}S) and the amount taken up was measured using a Geiger-Müller tube (counts per minute).

sulphate uptake/ counts per min / conditions	time/minutes								
	0	30	60	90	120	150	180	210	240
aerobic	0	210	300	355	400	450	490	510	540
anaerobic	0	100	195	205	210	230	260	280	295
the presence of a metabolic poison	0	100	170	190	200	205	215	230	250

(a) Use squared paper to plot, on the same axes, three curves to represent the data in the table. Label each of the curves. (5)

(b) A scientist suggested that uptake of sulphate ions by barley plants involved the process of **active transport**.
Using the information in the graph, describe the evidence that would support this suggestion. Explain why the evidence is supportive.

....

....

....

....

....

....

.... (5)

(c) (i) Sulphate ions can also move by diffusion.
Define diffusion in terms of the movement of these ions.

....

.... (1)

(ii) How would the results in the table have been different if the uptake of sulphate ions had resulted from simple diffusion alone?

....

.... (2)

MEG 1996

2 Humans

The **digestive system** breaks up the complex molecules in the food that we eat into simpler molecules that can be absorbed and used by our bodies. In the mouth, teeth chop and grind food into small particles and the enzyme amylase that is present in saliva starts to break down starch molecules into smaller sugar molecules. Food then passes down the **oesophagus** to the **stomach**. Here it is churned and mixed with stomach acid so that the proteases, protein-digesting enzymes that are also in the stomach, have the correct pH. The stomach acid also kills bacteria that are ingested with food. As the food next passes through the **small intestine**, kept moving along by **peristalsis**, bile is added from the liver. This breaks up fat into tiny droplets ready for lipases, enzymes added in the small intestine, to convert them into simpler substances. Useful chemicals pass into the blood by diffusion. In the **large intestine** water is absorbed into the blood and any undigested waste is then expelled from the anus as faeces.

The **circulatory system** passes blood round the body. Blood is pumped at high pressure from the heart through **arteries** to the lungs where carbon dioxide and water diffuse out of the blood and oxygen diffuses in. Blood then returns at lower pressure to the heart through **veins** before being pumped around the other body organs. Blood is a fluid called plasma that contains **red blood cells**, **white blood cells** and **platelets**. Red blood cells transport oxygen, white blood cells kill microbes and platelets form blood clots when the skin is cut. Carbon dioxide and the products of digestion are transported in the plasma.

The organs that make up the gas exchange system are in the **thorax**. Air is drawn into the lungs when they are expanded by the downward movement of the **diaphragm** and the outward movement of the **ribcage**. Air is forced out of the lungs when these movements are reversed. Exhaled air contains more carbon dioxide and water vapour, but less oxygen, than inhaled air. The proportion of nitrogen is the same for both exhaled air and inhaled air.

The lungs are damaged by the constant irritation of tobacco smoke. The delicate cell walls of the alveoli are damaged. Smoking reduces the efficiency of gas exchange and can cause lung cancer. Smoking during pregnancy reduces the amount of oxygen available to the developing fetus.

Oxygen from breathing, and glucose from digestion of food, are carried by the blood to all cells in the body. In **aerobic respiration** oxygen and carbohydrate react together; the reaction releases energy and produces carbon dioxide and water as waste. The waste products are transported back to the lungs by the blood. During vigorous exercise there may not be sufficient oxygen available so **anaerobic respiration** takes place, releasing less energy from the glucose and forming lactic acid as a waste product. This causes an 'oxygen debt' that has to be repaid; when there is sufficient oxygen available the lactic acid is oxidised to form carbon dioxide and water.

The body has receptors that detect changes in light, sound, position, taste, smell, pressure, balance and temperature. Impulses from these receptors travel to the **central nervous system** which is made up of the brain and spinal cord. These impulses can lead to two types of action – **reflex actions** and **conscious actions**. Reflex actions, such as removing a hand from a hot surface, occur very quickly and the impulses are sent by the most direct route through reflex arcs. Impulses for conscious actions take a longer route involving the brain where decisions are taken that initiate a response. This takes place more slowly.

A much slower way of sending messages round the body uses chemical messengers called **hormones**. The **endocrine system** consists of a number of glands that release hormones into the bloodstream. The hormones are then carried around the body until they reach the appropriate organ. Examples include:

hormone	produced in	effect of the hormone
growth hormone	pituitary gland	speeds up growth
insulin	pancreas	controls the amount of sugar in blood
female sex hormone	ovaries	controls menstrual cycle and sexual development

A diabetic person does not produce enough insulin to control the level of sugar in the blood. Regular injections of insulin are necessary to provide this control.

Fertility drugs contain a hormone that stimulates the release of eggs from the ovaries, while the contraceptive pill taken by females contains hormones that prevent the release of eggs.

The diagram shows the main parts of the **eye**.

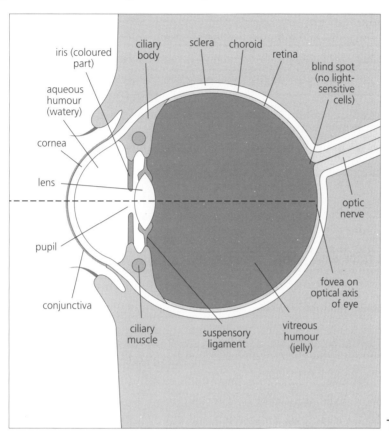

The eye

The **cornea** and **lens** together produce a focused image on the **retina**, where light-sensitive cells respond by sending electrical impulses along the optic nerve to the brain.

The internal environment of the body, eg temperature, concentration of water and other substances in the blood, needs to be kept constant for the body to function correctly. This is known as **homeostasis**. The **kidneys** remove urea and other poisonous substances from the blood. The water content of the blood is monitored by the brain; too little water in the blood causes the release of antidiurectic hormone (ADH) and the kidney responds by removing less water from the blood.

Blood temperature is also monitored by the brain. Excessive blood temperature leads to heat loss by **sweating** and an increase in the blood flow near the surface of the skin by **vasodilation**, a widening of the capillaries in the skin.

The body defends itself against bacteria and viruses in several ways. The skin is a barrier that they cannot penetrate; when there is a break in the skin the blood produces a clot to keep out bacteria and viruses. The mouth and nose also trap airborne bacteria and viruses in sticky mucus; when this is swallowed the bacteria and viruses are killed by the stomach acid. White blood cells can ingest microbes, produce antibodies to kill them or antitoxins to counter the effect of poisonous substances released by microbes into the blood.

Alcohol is a legal drug that slows down the reactions and can damage the liver and brain. It is particularly dangerous to undertake any activity that requires rapid response, such as driving, while under the influence of alcohol. Inhalation of organic solvents can have a dramatic effect on behaviour and cause permanent damage to essential organs.

If you need to revise this subject more thoroughly, see the relevant topics in the *Letts* GCSE Science Study Guide or CD-ROM.

1 The regulation of body temperature is achieved by balancing energy release against energy loss. Energy release is greater during exercise.

(a) The rate of metabolism changes during exercise. Describe how this influences energy release.

....

....

.... (2)

(b) Explain why, during exercise, the body attempts to lose more energy.

....

.... (2)

(c) During rest, excess blood sugar is stored. How is this achieved?

....

....

.... (2)

(d) The graphs show how the blood glucose level and the concentration of hormone involved in glucose storage vary over a 12-hour time period.

Key:
——— blood glucose
‒ ‒ ‒ concentration of hormone

quantity

8am 10am noon 2pm 4pm 6pm 8pm

time of day

(i) Using these graphs explain why a single daily dose of hormone would not adequately control blood glucose concentration in diabetics.

....

....

.... (2)

(ii) Explain how physical exercise would influence the production of the hormone involved in glucose storage.

....

....

.... (2)

MEG 1994

2 (a) Hydrochloric acid in the stomach helps in the digestion of food. Explain one other function of this substance in the stomach.

....

.... (2)

(b) The diagram shows a cross-section of a branch of a bronchus from a lung as seen with a microscope.

cilia

mucus-producing cell

air space

outer wall

(i) Use information from the diagram to help you to explain how the body is defended from disease-causing microorganisms which are present in air breathed into the body.

....

....

....

.... (4)

(ii) Mucus is produced by cells lining the nasal cavity. Explain what happens to this mucus in a healthy person.

....

.... (2)

(c) The chemicals in cigarette smoke can destroy the cilia at the top of the trachea.

(i) Explain why this often causes a thick fluid (phlegm) to collect in the trachea.

.... (1)

(ii) Why could this phlegm increase the risk of respiratory disease?

.... (1)

SEG 1995

3 Humans can survive in environments as hot as 50°C and as cold as –50°C. They are able to maintain a blood temperature between 36°C and 38°C. The table shows some of the possible responses to cold and heat.

responses to cold	responses to heat
increased voluntary movement	decreased voluntary movement
increased metabolic rate	reduced metabolic rate
shivering	sweating
putting on more clothing	taking off clothing
moving to a warmer place	moving to a colder place
vasoconstriction	vasodilation

(a) Explain how an increased metabolic rate can help to maintain blood temperature in a cold environment.

....

.... (2)

(b) Suggest why sweating has a greater cooling effect in a dry desert than in the humid tropics.

....

.... (2)

(c) Explain how vasoconstriction helps to maintain blood temperature in a cold environment.

....

....

.... (2)

(d) The diagram shows the principle of a homeostatic process.

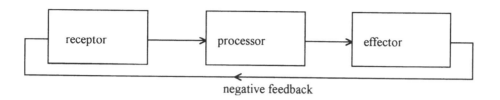

Use this diagram to explain how blood temperature can be maintained by shivering.

....

....

....

....

....

.... (4)

MEG 1996

3 Green plants as organisms

REVISION SUMMARY

Green plants make food by the process of photosynthesis. This can be summarised by the following equation:

$$\text{carbon dioxide} + \text{water} \rightarrow \text{glucose} + \text{oxygen}$$
$$6CO_2(g) + 6H_2O(l) \rightarrow C_6H_{12}O_6(aq) + 6O_2(g)$$

The carbon dioxide comes from the respiration of plant cells and also from the air and water around them. Chlorophyll, the green pigment present in the chloroplasts, is the catalyst for the process.

The rate of photosynthesis can be affected by a number of **limiting factors**. A limiting factor is something which restricts a process such as photosynthesis. Carbon dioxide concentration is a limiting factor. Up to a certain carbon dioxide concentration, increasing the concentration increases the rate of photosynthesis.

Above that concentration, increasing the concentration of carbon dioxide has no effect on the rate of photosynthesis.

Other limiting factors include light intensity, temperature and magnesium ion concentration. If the concentration of magnesium ions is too low, insufficient chlorophyll is made by the plant. This results eventually in the plant producing a low yield.

Plant cells can use the glucose and oxygen produced by photosynthesis for respiration. Some of the glucose is turned into sucrose and used by the shoot and root tips to promote their growth. Some sugar is used to produce nectar, fruits and seeds within the plant.

Surplus glucose is stored as starch. For example, starch is stored in the underground stems of potato plants. Glucose is the starting material for the manufacture of many different chemicals in the plant.

A healthy plant requires other essential elements. These include nitrogen, phosphorus, potassium, sulphur and magnesium. They are usually taken in through the roots in solution from the soil. A whole range of elements, called trace elements, are required in small amounts for specific processes.

Chemicals which regulate the growth and development of plants are called **plant growth substances** or **plant hormones**.

Commercial applications of plant hormones include rooting powders, selective weedkillers and in the production of seedless fruits.

Water is taken into a plant through the roots. Most of the water enters through specialised cells called root hair cells. These have a very large surface area to absorb water by the process of osmosis. The evaporation of water from the leaves into the atmosphere is called **transpiration**. The continuous flow of water through a plant is called the **transpiration stream**. Factors that affect the rate of transpiration include humidity, temperature, wind and light level.

Most of the water loss from a plant is lost through the stomata. The guard cells of the stomata are light sensitive; they open the stomata during periods of light and close the stomata during periods of darkness.

Plants are adapted to conserve water. The pressure of the water in plant cells keeps them rigid or turgid. Dead xylem cells form wood. This tissue provides the main supporting structure for woody plants such as trees. Turgid cells are important in supporting the plant; without turgor a plant may wilt.

Tissues that are involved in transporting substances required for growth and reproduction are concentrated in regions called **vascular bundles**. There are two types of tissue: **xylem** and **phloem**. Water passes along the xylem while the phloem carries nutrients such as sugars.

If you need to revise this subject more thoroughly, see the relevant topics in the *Letts* GCSE *Science Study Guide* or *CD-ROM*.

1 Leaves are organs of photosynthesis. They come in all shapes and sizes but all of them are adapted to absorb as much light as possible.

(a) Give **one** way in which leaves are adapted to absorb light.

.... (1)

(b) The diagram shows a cross-section through a leaf.

light

cuticle

chloroplast

palisade layer

spongy layer

air space

stomata

Explain the following observations:

(i) The cuticle is transparent.

.... (1)

(ii) Most chloroplasts are found in the palisade layer.

.... (1)

(iii) Air spaces are found mostly in the spongy layer.

.... (1)

(c) What is the substance in chloroplasts which absorbs light?

.... (1)

(d) Explain how each of the following affects the rate of photosynthesis in a potted plant.

(i) Moving it nearer to the window.

.... (1)

(ii) Moving it to a colder room.

.... (1)

(e) Complete the word equation for photosynthesis.

.... + water $\rightarrow$ carbohydrates + ... (1)

MEG 1994

2 A food store sells freshly picked peas. Some were grown in Britain and some in Zimbabwe in Africa. Pea plants need 17 hours of daylight each day to produce a high yield of sweet, tasty peas. Zimbabwe has only 12 hours of daylight each day. In Zimbabwe, floodlights are switched on in the pea fields as soon as it becomes dark.

(a) What are the advantages of using floodlights in the pea fields?

....

....

....

....

.... (4)

(b) The amount of carbon dioxide in the air around the pea plants was measured during two different days (day **X** and day **Y**). On one of these days, the floodlights were not used because there was a power cut.
The graph below shows the amounts of carbon dioxide around the pea plants on day **X** and day **Y**.

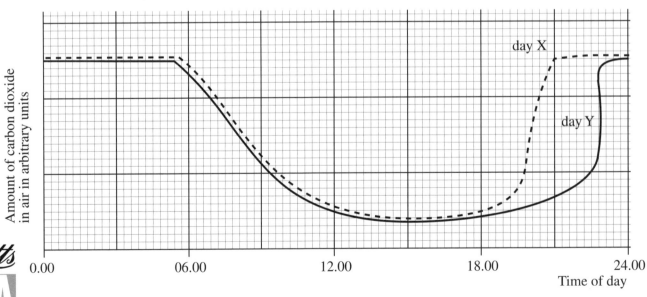

Use the information in the graph to answer the questions below.

  (i) At what time of day did the pea plants use most carbon dioxide?

      .... (1)

  (ii) On which day, day **X** or day **Y**, was there a power cut?
      Give a reason for your answer.

      ....

      .... (2)

(c) Suggest **two** factors, other than light and carbon dioxide, which could help the growth of pea plants.

1 ....

2 .... (2)

(d) Peas can be tested for the presence of simple sugar.
    The list below includes stages in the test.

    A Add Benedict's solution.

    B Colour changes from blue to brick red.

    C Colour changes from brick red to blue.

    D Heat the test tube.

    E Place peas in a test tube with water.

    Give the order of stages in a **positive** test by writing **one** letter in each box in the table below. The first stage has been done for you.

Order of stages	Letter
1	**E**
2	
3	
4	

(3)

Edexcel 1998

4 Variation, inheritance and evolution

The offspring of sexually reproducing organisms are not identical. These differences are called **variation**.

There are two types of variation – continuous variation (e.g. height) and discontinuous variation (e.g. blood group or sex). Continuous variation produces a normal distribution curve. With discontinuous variation there are only certain discrete possibilities with no 'in-betweens'.

The characteristics of an individual are inherited from its parents. The genes present in the sperm and egg determine the genetic character of the offspring. Whether an individual reaches its full potential depends upon environmental factors such as availability of food.

While sexual reproduction produces variation, asexual reproduction, e.g. taking a cutting of a geranium, produces identical offspring. The genetic information in the geranium and the cutting is the same. Offspring with identical genetic information are called **clones**.

Variation can also be caused by **mutations**. If the copying process that occurs when cells undergo meiosis is faulty, the genes produced will be different. They are called **mutant genes** and the process is called **mutation**. Mutations occur naturally and not all mutations are bad. The rate at which mutations occur can be speeded up by specific environmental agents called **mutagens**. Ionising radiation and particular chemicals can act as mutagens.

We inherit characteristics from our parents. The study of the way in which we inherit these characteristics is called **genetics**. Information is passed on by **genes**. A gene is a section of **DNA** (**deoxyribonucleic acid**) **polymer**. A number of these genes make up the **chromosomes** which are found in the **nucleus of a cell**. In a human all cells (apart from sex cells) contain 46 chromosomes arranged in 23 **homologous pairs**.

There are two ways in which cell division can occur – **mitosis** and **meiosis**. In mitosis exact copies of cells are produced (see Chapter 1). Mitosis occurs when an organism grows and when an organism reproduces asexually, forming **clones**.

Sex cells (eggs and sperm) are produced by meiosis. These cells contain half the number of chromosomes of a normal cell. In a human there are 23 chromosomes in each sex cell. In **fertilisation** 23 chromosomes from the mother combine with 23 chromosomes from the father. The offspring contains 46 chromosomes (23 pairs), with half coming from the mother and half from the father.

The sex of a baby is determined by a pair of sex chromosomes. There are two types of sex chromosome.

❶ The long **X** chromosome.   ❷ The short **Y** chromosome.

The cells in a female contain two **X** chromosomes (**XX**) and in a male the cells contain one **X** and one **Y** chromosome (**XY**). The diagram shows how males and females are produced.

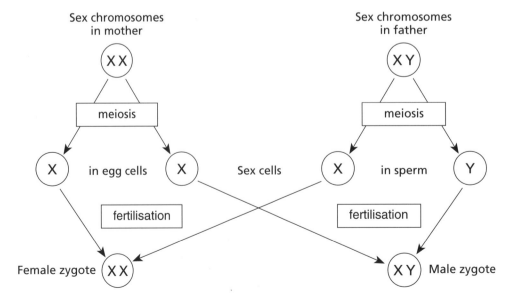

A particular characteristic may be determined by a single gene. A gene may exist in more than one form, each known as an allele. One allele in a zygote has come from the mother and one from the father. One of the alleles may be **dominant** and the other may be **recessive**. If a dominant allele is present, it results in one particular characteristic. If two recessive alleles are present then a different characteristic will be shown.

Eye colour is determined genetically. For example, two alleles may be **B** (the dominant allele which produces brown eyes) and **b** (the recessive allele which produces blue eyes). There are three possible combinations of alleles (called **genotypes**) **BB**, **Bb** (or **bB**) and **bb**. A child who inherits the genotypes **BB** or **Bb** has brown eyes because of the presence of the dominant **B** allele and a child who inherits the genotype **bb** has blue eyes.

Genotypes which contain two identical alleles (e.g. **BB** or **bb**) are said to be **homozygous**. Genotypes which contain two different alleles are called **heterozygous**. The diagrams, called Punnett squares, summarise what happens when parents with different eye colour have children.

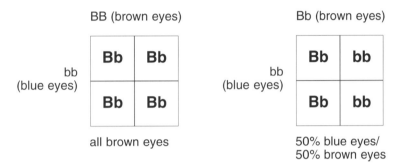

Different genes control other characteristics in the same way. In some cases, however, the gene which controls a characteristic is not present in the shorter **Y** chromosome. In the male there is only one gene present (on the **X** chromosome) and this alone determines the characteristic. Some conditions, such as colour blindness and haemophilia, are sex-linked and occur predominantly in males because the gene is recessive on the **X** chromosome. Other conditions, such as cystic fibrosis, are produced by a recessive gene which can show equally in males and females.

Selective breeding is used by scientists to improve the desirable characteristics in plants and animals. This requires identification of the characteristic which needs to be improved, e.g. yield, fat-to-lean ratio in a meat carcase. Parents are chosen which show the characteristic required and breeding takes place. Offspring are chosen which show the characteristic required and the process is repeated.

Genetic engineering involves the replacement of one gene from a chromosome with another gene from another organism which has improved characteristics. In an attempt to produce a true blue rose, scientists are replacing the gene which causes colour in the rose by the gene which makes petunia flowers blue. This process has also been used to produce antibiotics and hormones.

Evolution is a theory about how organisms present on the Earth today came to be there.

Evidence for evolution can be obtained by studying **fossils**. Fossils are the remains of plants and animals that have been preserved rather than decomposed.

Variation can lead to new organisms which are better adapted for their environment. This change over many generations can lead to changes in organisms due to **natural selection**. Over many generations failure to adapt to the changing environment may cause some species to become **extinct**.

If you need to revise this subject more thoroughly, see the relevant topics in the *Letts* GCSE Science Study Guide or CD-ROM.

1 The table shows how the average milk yield per Ayrshire cow increased between 1807 and 1967.

Year	Average yield of milk per cow (litres per year)
1807	1934
1855	2570
1955	3567
1967	4004

(a) Explain, as fully as you can, how farmers might have increased the amount of milk yielded by cows.

....

....

....

.... (3)

(b) Give **two** advantages in having cows which produce higher yields of milk.

....

.... (2)

NEAB 1994

2 The peppered moth has light-coloured wings 'peppered' with dark spots and bars. In 1850 a dark variety of this moth, with almost black wings, was discovered in Manchester. After 1850, the dark form rapidly became more and more common, so that today, in the Manchester area, the light-coloured variety is rare. The light-coloured variety still continues to thrive in some other parts of the United Kingdom.

(a) Suggest how the original dark-coloured variety came into existence.

....

....

.... (2)

(b) Explain why the dark-coloured variety has now become the common variety in the Manchester area.

....

.... (2)

SEG 1994

3 (a) Complete the diagram below to show how the sex of a child depends on the chromosomes the child inherits.

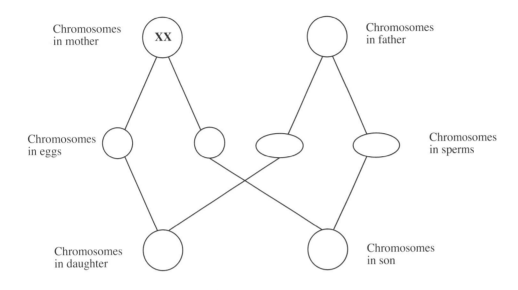

(3)

(b) The diagram below shows the inheritance of Huntington's chorea in a family.

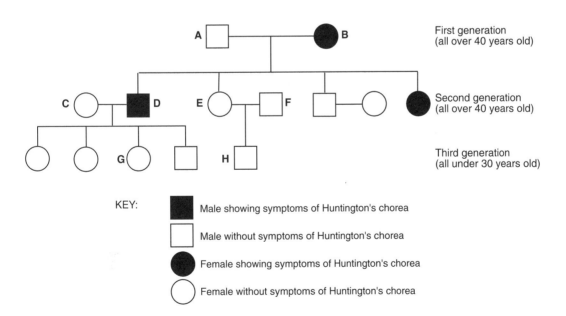

First generation
(all over 40 years old)

Second generation
(all over 40 years old)

Third generation
(all under 30 years old)

KEY:

■ Male showing symptoms of Huntington's chorea

□ Male without symptoms of Huntington's chorea

● Female showing symptoms of Huntington's chorea

○ Female without symptoms of Huntington's chorea

Symptoms of Huntington's chorea usually develop between the ages of 35 and 40.

What is the chance that the following will develop Huntington's chorea?

G ....

H ....

Explain the reasons for your answers as fully as you can. You may use genetic diagrams if you wish.

....

....

....

....

....

....

.... (6)

NEAB 1995

The population of living organisms can increase very rapidly. The sketch graph shows the usual exponential increase of a typical population of organisms, e.g. animals, plants, bacteria, etc.

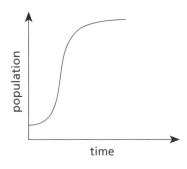

The growth of a population slows down due to

● competition for food and living space;

● build up of toxic wastes;

● introduction of **predators**.

Birth rate and death rate are expressed as yearly percentages, and are used to calculate population growth. A birth rate of 15% means that for every 100 individuals at the beginning of the year, there are 15 more at the end of the year (i.e. 115). A death rate of 5% means that for every 100 individuals at the beginning of the year, there would be 5 less at the end of the year (i.e. 95). This population would show an increase of $15 - 5 = 10\%$.

The increase of the human population has led to an increase in the exploitation of raw materials. Industry and farming have led to an increase in the use of raw materials. Industry and farming produce goods and food on a massive scale. This has benefits for the population in the form of jobs leading to prosperity and a higher standard of living. However, there is a detrimental effect on the environment. There are increasing problems concerning the

● disposal of our waste;

● pollution of rivers, lakes and seas;

● extensive use of fertilisers causing **eutrophication** of water systems;

● reduction of tropical rain forests.

This increase in development has caused a change in the **biosphere**. The biosphere is that part of the Earth and its atmosphere which is inhabited by living things.

The increase in carbon dioxide in the air has led to the **greenhouse effect**, which causes global warming.

CFCs (chlorofluorocarbons) are released into the atmosphere causing holes to be formed in the **ozone layer** in the upper atmosphere. The ozone layer protects us on the Earth from the harmful ultraviolet rays which can cause skin cancer.

Acid rain is due to the increase in sulphur dioxide and nitrogen oxides being emitted into the atmosphere from the burning of fossil fuels. These gases react with water in the atmosphere to produce sulphuric and nitric acids. The acids will then react with metals and some rocks (e.g. limestone) and reduce the pH of water in rivers and lakes.

Only a small amount of the Sun's energy that falls onto a plant is transferred into the plant's tissues and food stores. When a rabbit eats the plant only about one-tenth of the energy in the plant is transferred to the body of the rabbit. The rest of the energy is lost as the rabbit moves, respires, through excretion and body heat. The same principle applies when a rabbit is eaten by a fox.

Energy flow in a food chain can be expressed in a pyramid of numbers and a pyramid of biomass. As there is a loss of energy at each level of the food chain, the number of organisms that can be supported at each level becomes less. This drop in numbers at each level of a food chain is expressed as a **pyramid of numbers**. This drop in numbers of organisms can also be

REVISION SUMMARY

expressed as a reduction in the total mass of living material at each level. This is called the **pyramid of biomass**.

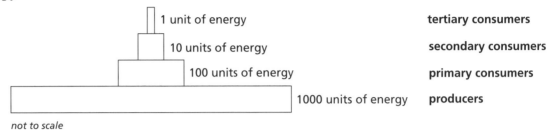

1 unit of energy	**tertiary consumers**
10 units of energy	**secondary consumers**
100 units of energy	**primary consumers**
1000 units of energy	**producers**

not to scale

Carbon and nitrogen are important elements that are **recycled** naturally. Within the **carbon cycle** photosynthesis is the only process that removes carbon dioxide from the atmosphere. Carbon dioxide is returned to the atmosphere during the processes of **combustion**, **respiration** and **decay**.

Plants cannot use the element nitrogen from the atmosphere; nitrogen-fixing bacteria convert nitrogen in the air into useful nitrogen compounds in the soil. Plants absorb nitrates and turn them into amino acids, which are used to build up proteins. Nitrogen is also returned to the soil by lightning, decaying plants and animals and excretion.

Decay enables chemicals to be **recycled**. There are three main groups of **decomposers** – **bacteria**, **fungi** and **soil invertebrates**. The conditions necessary for decay are **warmth**, **moisture** and **oxygen**. Decay is an important process in the treatment of sewage and the formation of compost.

With the need for more food, **intensive farming** methods were introduced. Small fields were combined to form large fields. Large machinery then made farming more efficient. Removal of hedges removed the habitat of some plants and animals and soil erosion increased.

Ecosystems need to be correctly managed to prevent environmental damage. Intensive farming methods and overgrazing can cause soil erosion. Tropical rainforests are an example of an ecosystem managed incorrectly. The deforestation has ruined the soil, encouraged flooding and soil erosion, and caused changes to the local climate. It has also killed wildlife on a massive scale and increased the concentration of carbon dioxide in the atmosphere, contributing to the greenhouse effect.

It has become necessary to conserve ecosystems to prevent the loss of unique areas, such as wetlands and rainforests, thus hopefully preventing the extinction of endangered species. The Government has enforced conservation of marine stocks by introducing fishing quotas and regulations on the mesh sizes of nets. This hopefully ensures we do not remove fish faster than they can be replaced by the natural process of reproduction.

If you need to revise this subject more thoroughly, see the relevant topics in the *Letts* **GCSE** *Science Study Guide* **or** *CD-ROM*.

1 The diagram below shows a grassland food web. Numbers on arrows show the energy available to organisms, in kJ per m² per year. Numbers in brackets show the energy that becomes part of the biomass of the organisms, in kJ per m² per year.

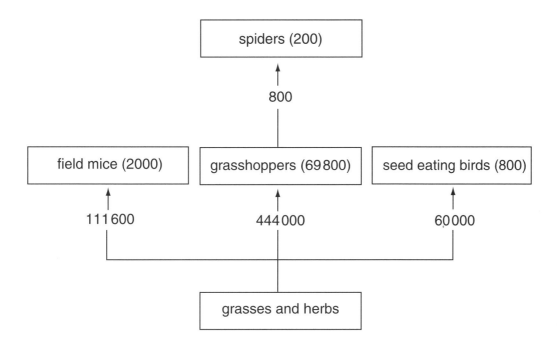

The energy efficiency of an organism is a measure of how much of the energy available to the organism becomes part of its biomass.
The equation below shows how to calculate energy efficiency.

$$\text{energy efficiency (\%)} = \frac{\text{energy that becomes part of biomass}}{\text{energy available}} \times 100$$

(a) (i) Calculate the energy efficiency of spiders.
Put your answer in the table below.

Organism	Energy efficiency as %
field mice	1.8
grasshoppers	15.7
seed eating birds	1.3
spiders	

(1)

Letts

Q&A

(ii) Suggest **one** reason why field mice are less energy efficient than grasshoppers.

....

.... (1)

(b) (i) How much energy available to the birds did not become part of their biomass?

Answer .... kJ per m² per year (1)

(ii) Explain what has happened to the energy that was available to the birds but did not become part of their biomass.

....

....

.... (2)

Edexcel 1998

2 (a) The diagram shows three possible pathways by which the energy captured by green plants may be passed on to humans.

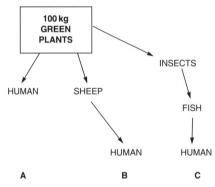

(i) Which of the pathways **A**, **B** or **C** would allow **most** energy from the plants to be available to humans? Explain your answer.

....

.... (2)

(ii) Which of the pathways **A**, **B** or **C** would be typical of starving populations? Explain your answer.

....

.... (2)

(iii) In which of the pathways **A**, **B** or **C** is most energy lost as heat? Explain your answer.

....

....

.... (2)

(b) (i) Look at the following food chain:

rose bush → aphids (greenflies) → ladybirds

Explain why the pyramid of **biomass** for this food chain would be a different shape from the pyramid of **numbers**.

....

....

.... (2)

(ii) The graph shows how the numbers of greenfly and ladybirds fluctuated over the Summer period during a year in which two of the weeks in July were hot and humid. This resulted in an abnormally high population of greenfly.

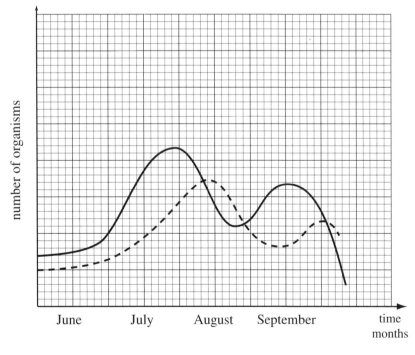

——————— greenfly population

– – – – – ladybird population

Explain the form of the graph.

....

....

....

.... (2)

(iii) Ladybirds control the number of greenfly on rose bushes.
Why is this natural method preferable to the use of insecticide sprays?

....

....

....

.... (2)

MEG 1997

REVISION SUMMARY

There are three states of matter – **solid**, **liquid** and **gas**. All matter can exist in any of these states depending upon conditions of temperature and pressure. In all three states the material is made up of particles

In a solid the particles are vibrating about fixed positions. If the solid is crystalline the particles are regularly arranged and usually closely packed. In a liquid the particles are still close together but there is no regular arrangement. There is more movement of particles and the movement gets more as temperature rises. In the gas state the particles have broken away from each other and are free to move around.

When a change of state occurs, e.g. solid to liquid, there is an associated energy change. In this case energy is required to break up the solid structure and give the particles additional kinetic energy. The reverse process – liquid to solid – will release energy. **Diffusion** is the movement of particles to spread out and fill all of the available space. Diffusion takes place rapidly with gases because the particles in a gas are moving rapidly. It takes place more slowly in liquids and solids because there is less movement of particles.

Elements are composed of atoms. A piece of iron is made up solely of iron atoms. In a mixture there will be different types of atom and the atoms of the different elements will not be joined. In a compound again there will be atoms of different elements but they will be joined together. A mixture of hydrogen and oxygen can consist of hydrogen and oxygen in different proportions but water, a compound of hydrogen and oxygen, contains always twice as many atoms of hydrogen as oxygen. Groups of atoms in elements or compounds are called molecules. An oxygen molecule consists of a pair of oxygen atoms together, O_2, and a water molecule two hydrogen atoms and one oxygen, H_2O.

Atoms of the different elements are made up of different numbers of protons, neutrons and electrons. An atom always contains an equal number of protons and electrons. If an atom loses one or more electrons it forms a **positive ion** or **cation**. If an atom gains one or more electrons it forms a **negative ion** or **anion**. Atoms of the same element must contain the same number of protons and electrons but can contain different numbers of neutrons. These are called **isotopes**. The protons and neutrons make up the positively charged nucleus and the electrons move around the nucleus.

There are two methods commonly used to join or **bond** atoms together. **Ionic bonding**, e.g. sodium chloride, involves the complete transfer of one or more electrons from a metal atom to a non metal atom. This forms ions which are held together by strong electrostatic forces. **Covalent bonding**, e.g. chlorine or hydrogen chloride, involves the sharing of pairs of electrons.

The properties of a material are related to the structure of the material. If the material is made up of molecules it will have a low melting and boiling point. If it is made up of a giant structure of atoms or ions, it will have a high melting point. A giant structure of ions produces a melt which conducts electricity.

Chemical reactions which release energy are called **exothermic** reactions and ones which take in energy are called **endothermic** reactions. These can be represented in energy level diagrams.

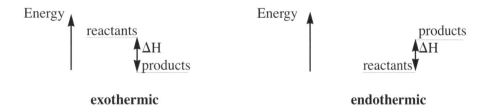

exothermic   endothermic

When chemical bonds are broken, energy is used, and energy is produced when bonds are formed. If a reaction is exothermic (gives out energy) the energy produced by bonds formed is greater than the energy required to break the bonds.

If you need to revise this subject more thoroughly, see the relevant topics in the *Letts* GCSE *Science Study Guide* or CD-ROM.

QUESTIONS

1   The diagrams show simple representations of hydrogen and bromine.

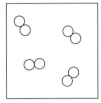
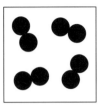

hydrogen   bromine

(a) In these diagrams, in which state are hydrogen and bromine?

.... (1)

(b) What do each of the following diagrams represent? Add suitable captions to the diagrams.

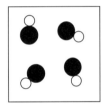
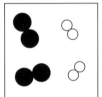
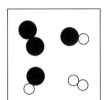

....

....

....

....

.... (3)

(c) (i) Draw a diagram to show the bonding in a hydrogen bromide gas molecule. Show only the outer electrons. What type of bonding is present in the molecule?   (3)

Type of bonding ....

(ii) A damp thermometer is placed into a gas jar containing dry hydrogen bromide gas. The temperature shown on the thermometer rises. Suggest what changes occur to the hydrogen bromide when water is added.

....

....

.... (3)

2 The table below shows some information about the isotopes of chlorine.

(a) Use information from the Periodic Table to help you complete the table.

Isotope	Mass Number	Abundance	Number of protons in one atom	Number of electrons in one atom	Number of neutrons in one atom
chlorine-35		75%			
chlorine-37		25%			

(4)

(b) (i) Show why the relative atomic mass of chlorine is given as 35.5.

....

....

....

.... (2)

(ii) What is the relative molecular mass of a chlorine molecule?

.... (1)

(c) Draw a dot and cross diagram for a molecule of chlorine, showing outer electrons only.

(2)

(d) State **one** use of chlorine, apart from water purification.

.... (1)

Edexcel 1998

3 (a) Substances may be classified in terms of their properties as having a metallic, ionic, covalent molecular or giant covalent structure.
Complete the table below for the substances given.

Substance	Structure	Melting point	Electrical conductivity	
			Solid	Molten
diamond	giant covalent	high	poor	
magnesium chloride	ionic	high		good
bromine		low	poor	poor

(3)

(b) Draw a diagram to show the arrangement of **outer** shell electrons in a water molecule.

(2)
NICCEA 1998

The study of the chemistry of carbon compounds, excluding some simple compounds such as carbon dioxide and carbon monoxide, is called **organic chemistry**. There are a very large number of carbon compounds because of the stable bonds formed by carbon atoms with other carbon atoms and with atoms of a range of other elements.

Petroleum (crude oil) is a source of hydrocarbons widely used in the chemical industry. Fractional distillation separates petroleum into different fractions, each containing a number of chemical compounds which boil within a range of temperature.

Most of the compounds making up petroleum are **alkanes**. These are a homologous series of **hydrocarbons** (compounds of carbon and hydrogen only) which all fit a general formula of C_nH_{2n+2}. The simplest members are:

$$
\begin{array}{ccccc}
\text{H} & \text{H H} & \text{H H H} & \text{H H H H} & \text{H H H} \\
\mid & \mid\ \mid & \mid\ \mid\ \mid & \mid\ \mid\ \mid\ \mid & \mid\ \mid\ \mid \\
\text{H--C--H} & \text{H--C--C--H} & \text{H--C--C--C--H} & \text{H--C--C--C--C--H} & \text{H--C--C--C--H} \\
\mid & \mid\ \mid & \mid\ \mid\ \mid & \mid\ \mid\ \mid\ \mid & \mid\quad\mid \\
\text{H} & \text{H H} & \text{H H H} & \text{H H H H} & \text{H--C--H} \\
 & & & & \mid \\
 & & & & \text{H}
\end{array}
$$

| CH_4 | C_2H_6 | C_3H_8 | C_4H_{10} | |
| methane | ethane | propane | n-butane | isobutane |

There are two **isomers** of butane because alternative arrangements of the atoms are possible. All alkanes are **saturated**, i.e. they contain only carbon–carbon single bonds. Alkanes make good fuels, but are otherwise unreactive.

Cracking is used to break long-chain alkanes into smaller molecules. The products of cracking depend upon conditions. Some of the molecules produced are **unsaturated** and belong to the homologous series of **alkenes**. Alkenes fit a general formula C_nH_{2n} and contain a carbon–carbon double bond. The simplest alkene is ethene, C_2H_4. The presence of a carbon–carbon double bond (or triple bond) can be detected by using bromine dissolved in a suitable solvent (e.g. hexane). The bromine solution turns from red-brown to colourless.

Alkenes are much more reactive than alkanes. Like alkanes they burn, but they also take part in addition reactions, e.g.

ethene + hydrogen → ethane   ethene + water → ethanol

Manufacturing margarine is an important industrial process which uses the addition of hydrogen to unsaturated molecules. Animal and vegetable oils, the raw material, contain carbon–carbon double bonds and are liquid. The corresponding saturated compounds are suitable for use as margarine as they are solid. Hydrogen gas is passed through the oil in the presence of a nickel catalyst at 140 °C. Hydrogenation (reaction with hydrogen takes place).

Ethanol (sometimes called alcohol) can be produced from ethene by an addition reaction. It can also be produced by **fermentation**. Fermentation is the action of enzymes on a solution of sugar or starch.

$$C_6H_{12}O_6 \rightarrow 2C_2H_5OH + 2CO_2$$
glucose   ethanol   carbon dioxide

The solution produced by fermentation is a dilute solution of ethanol in water. The ethanol can be made more concentrated by fractional distillation.

REVISION SUMMARY

Many of the items which used to be made from metals are now made of plastic materials called **polymers**. There are many polymers which exist in nature, e.g. cellulose, starch and proteins. They are called **natural polymers**. Probably more important to us today for manufacturing items are factory-made **synthetic polymers**. Examples are poly(ethene), polystyrene and nylon.

Polymers are made up from very long chain molecules. These long chains are made up by joining together many smaller molecules called monomers. There can be between 1000 and 50 000 monomer molecules linked together in a polymer chain. The polymerisation process can be summarised by

$$H_2N - \boxed{} - NH_2 \qquad HOOC - \bigcirc - COOH \qquad \longrightarrow$$

hexane-1,6-diamine hexanedioic acid

$$\cdots\cdots\cdots - \overset{\overset{\displaystyle O}{\|}}{C} - NH - \boxed{} - NH - \overset{\overset{\displaystyle O}{\|}}{C} - \bigcirc - \overset{\overset{\displaystyle O}{\|}}{C} - NH - \boxed{} - NH - \overset{\overset{\displaystyle O}{\|}}{C} - \bigcirc - \cdots\cdots\cdots$$

In addition polymerisation the monomers contain a carbon–carbon double bond. The molecules join together without losing any atoms.

$$n\text{M} \rightarrow (\text{M})_n$$

An example of addition polymerisation is making poly(ethene).

$$n \left(\begin{array}{c} H \\ \diagdown \\ H \end{array} C = C \begin{array}{c} H \\ \diagup \\ H \end{array} \right) \longrightarrow \left[\begin{array}{cc} H & H \\ | & | \\ -C - C- \\ | & | \\ H & H \end{array} \right]_n$$

The polymer does not contain the double bond present in the monomer.

If you need to revise this subject more thoroughly, see the relevant topics in the *Letts* GCSE *Science Study Guide* or CD-ROM.

1 The diagram summarises how some important materials can be made from methane.

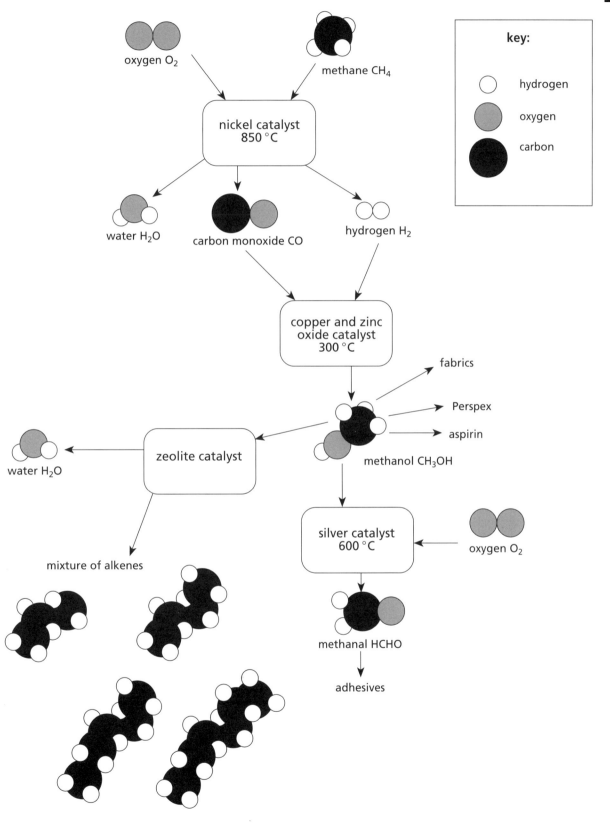

(a) What is an important source of methane for industry?

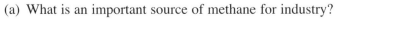

.... (1)

(b) The nickel catalyst has to be heated to 850 °C to start the reaction between oxygen and methane. After this, heating is not necessary and the catalyst reaction remains unchanged. What does this suggest about the reaction of methane and oxygen?

.... (1)

(c) What type of reaction is the conversion of methanol into methanal?

.... (1)

(d) A zeolite structure is very open with lots of tiny holes through it.
Why does this help a zeolite to be a good catalyst?

.... (1)

(e) Write a balanced symbolic equation for the formation of methanol.

.... (2)

(f) Suggest a use for the mixture of alkenes produced.

.... (1)

2 Crude oil is a mixture of many compounds. The diagram below shows some of the processes that take place in a petrochemical plant.

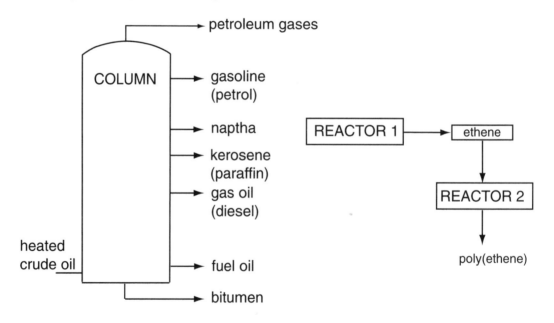

(a) Name the process which takes place in the COLUMN.

.... (1)

(b) Name the type of reactions which take place in:

    (i) REACTOR 1 ....

    (ii) REACTOR 2 .... (2)

(c) The petroleum gases contain ethane, C_2H_6 and propane, C_3H_8.
The structure of a molecule of ethane can be represented as:

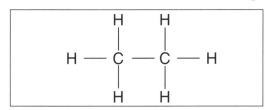 ethane

Draw the structure of a molecule of propane in the space below.

propane   (1)

(d) Ethane and propane are said to be *saturated* hydrocarbons.
What does *saturated* mean when used to describe hydrocarbons?

.... (1)

(e) Many molecules of ethene join together to form poly(ethene) in REACTOR 2.
Complete the diagram below to show the formation of poly(ethene).

(2)
NEAB 1997

REVISION SUMMARY

There are three parts which make up the Earth – the **crust**, the **mantle** and the **core**. The crust is a thin layer of surface rocks, between 7 km and 40 km thick. Underneath the crust is the mantle and in the centre of the Earth is the core. Our understanding of the structure of the core comes from studies including the passage of sound waves through the Earth. These studies, called seismic studies, show scientists that the inner core of the Earth is solid.

The work of Alfred Wegener (1880–1930) showed that the Earth's crust is made up from a number of huge **plates** which are floating on the liquid magma. Originally the plates made up one supercontinent called the Pangaea. These plates are moving very slowly – perhaps only a few centimetres a year. The movement of these plates is called **plate tectonics**.

Where two plates are sliding past each other, they produce stresses and strains which may be released suddenly in an **earthquake**. When two plates are moving apart, a crack will appear in the Earth's crust. Molten rock from the mantle will come to the surface and new rocks will be formed. This often takes place under oceans and is not easily seen. This is called a **constructive plate margin**.

When two plates collide, rocks are squeezed together. This causes the pushing of one plate upwards to create a mountain range. The Himalayas were formed from the collision of the Eurasian and Indian plates. Alternatively one of the plates is pushed back downwards into the magma. This is called a **destructive plate margin**.

The rocks of the Earth can be classified as igneous, metamorphic and sedimentary.

- **Igneous rocks** are formed when molten magma from inside the Earth is cooled. They are crystalline and the size of the crystals depends upon the rate of cooling. Large crystals are formed when the cooling is slow. There are two types of igneous rocks – **intrusive** rocks (e.g. granite), which are formed inside the Earth, and **extrusive** rocks (e.g. basalt), which are formed on the surface of the Earth.

- **Metamorphic rocks** are formed when high temperatures and pressures act on sedimentary and igneous rocks. Marble is a metamorphic rock produced from limestone.

- **Sedimentary rocks** are formed when rocks in the Earth are eroded and the sediments are transported and deposited. When these layers of rock fragments are compressed over a long period, sedimentary rocks are formed. Chalk is a sedimentary rock.

Rocks are being continuously recycled in the rock cycle.

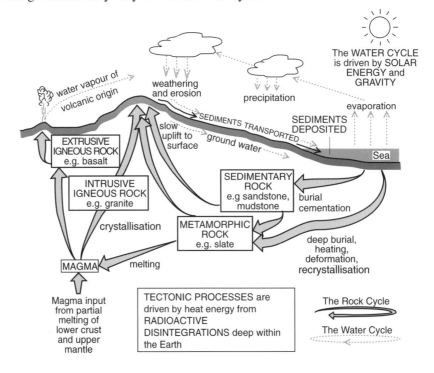

Rocks are used for a wide range of purposes – for building materials and as a source of raw material for making useful products. Metals are extracted from metal ores. The method of extraction is related to the reactivity of the metal.

Most metals react with oxygen, water and acids, but at different rates. Metals are often arranged in order of reactivity, called a **reactivity series**.

Such a series is:

K   Na   Ca   Mg   Al   Zn   Fe   Pb   Cu   Ag

decreasing reactivity

A reactivity series can be used to predict the products of a chemical reaction.

e.g. copper(II) sulphate + iron → copper + iron(II) sulphate

A reaction takes place because iron is more reactive than copper (higher in the reactivity series).

Metals high in the reactivity series are extracted from their ores by electrolysis.
Electrolysis involves the **decomposition** of an **electrolyte** using electricity. Electrolysis takes place when ions are free to move when an electrolyte is molten or dissolved in water. The products of electrolysis are formed at the electrodes.

e.g. lead(II) bromide (molten) → lead   +   bromine
                              (formed at the negative   (formed at the positive
                              electrode called the   electrode called the
                              cathode)   anode)

Metals and hydrogen are usually produced at the cathode and oxygen or one of the halogens at the anode. Ionic equations are often used to represent changes taking place at the electrodes.

Cathode: $Pb^{2+} + 2e^- \rightarrow Pb$ Anode: $2Br^- \rightarrow Br_2 + 2e^-$

Metals in the middle of the reactivity series are usually extracted by reduction of the ore with carbon. Metals low in the reactivity series are often found uncombined in the Earth or are extracted simply by heating.

Questions on the extraction of the metals aluminium and iron are frequently asked on GCSE Chemistry papers.

Extraction of aluminium

Bauxite is the ore of aluminium. It contains hydrated aluminium oxide Al_2O_3 $3H_2O$. The ore is purified to produce alumina – pure aluminium oxide, Al_2O_3. Aluminium is high in the reactivity series and aluminium oxide is difficult to split up. Electrolysis has to be used.

Aluminium is obtained by the electrolysis of alumina dissolved in molten cryolite (sodium aluminium fluoride, Na_3AlF_6). The anode and cathode are made of carbon.

The electrode reactions taking place are:

Cathode: $Al^{3+} + 3e^- \rightarrow Al$
Anode $2O^{2-} \rightarrow O_2 + 4e^-$

The carbon anode burns in the oxygen produced and has to be regularly replaced. Aluminium is tapped off from the cells.

The process takes a great deal of electricity. To produce 1 tonne of aluminium requires 17000 kW of electricity, enough electricity for the consumption of a good sized town for 1 hour.

Extraction of iron

Iron is extracted in a continuous process in a blast furnace. The blast furnace is loaded with iron ore (haematite, Fe_2O_3), coke and limestone. The furnace is heated with blasts of hot air.
The reactions taking place are:

   1. $C + O_2 \rightarrow CO_2$
   2. $CO_2 + C \rightarrow 2CO$
   3. $Fe_2O_3 + 3CO \rightarrow 2Fe + 3CO_2$
   4. $CaCO_3 \rightarrow CaO + CO_2$
   5. $CaO + SiO_2 \rightarrow CaSiO_3$

**REVISION
SUMMARY**

**If you need to
revise this
subject more
thoroughly,
see the relevant
topics in the
Letts GCSE
*Science
Study Guide* or
CD-ROM.**

In the important step 3 iron(III) oxide is reduced to iron by carbon monoxide. Impurities such as silicon dioxide are removed from the furnace in step 5 where basic and acidic oxides react to form calcium silicate which is called slag.

Molten impure iron (called pig iron) and molten slag are tapped off at the bottom of the furnace.

Most of the pig iron produced is turned into steel. In the steel making process, oxygen gas is blown through molten iron to convert impurities such as carbon, sulphur and phosphorus into acidic oxides, which escape as gases or react with added calcium oxide. Scrap iron can be added to the steel making furnace to reduce the amount of pig iron required. Finally carbon can be added to produce steel with the required specification.

Steel is an **alloy** of iron i.e. a mixture of iron with small quantities of carbon and possibly other metals. The addition of small quantities of other metals or carbon alters the properties of iron. High carbon steel, is strong but brittle. Low carbon steel is soft and is easily shaped. Stainless steel, which contains chromium and nickel, is hard and resistant to corrosion.

1 An underwater ridge called the Mid-Atlantic Ridge runs along the floor of the Atlantic Ocean. The age of the oldest sea floor sediments has been estimated at different distances from this ridge. The table below shows the results.

Distance from ridge/km	Age of oldest sediments/millions of years
250	10
500	26
750	38
1500	75

(a) Use this information to plot a graph showing how the age of the oldest sediments on the floor of the Atlantic Ocean depends on the distance from the Mid-Atlantic Ridge. (4)

You will need a square piece of graph paper (80 small squares on x and y axes)

(b) (i) Explain how the graph can be used to estimate the rate at which the ocean floor has spread apart in the past.

....

....

.... (1)

(ii) Use your graph to estimate the age of the oldest sediments 1000 km from the ridge.

....

.... (1)

(c) The spreading apart of the ocean floor on either side of the ridge can be explained by the theory of plate tectonics. According to the theory, materials near the ridge move as shown in the diagram.

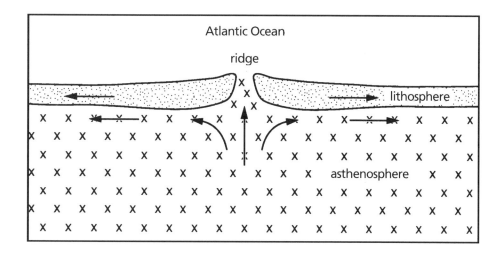

How can the theory of plate tectonics explain the formation of volcanoes at ocean ridges?

....

....

....

.... (4)

(d) A link has been suggested between the extinction of dinosaurs and a decrease in volcanic activity about 65 million years ago. Volcanoes release large quantities of carbon dioxide gas.
Suggest why scientists believe this change might have led to the extinction of dinosaurs.

....

....

....

.... (2)

MEG 1994

2 Iron is extracted from iron ore in blast furnace.

The furnace is loaded with iron ore, Fe_2O_3, coke, C, and limestone, $CaCO_3$.
Preheated air is blown into the furnace.
Molten iron and liquid slag are tapped from the bottom of the furnace.
The iron is approximately 95% pure and is taken to a nearby steel-making plant.
Hot waste gases containing 20% carbon monoxide come off at the top of the furnace.

One of the reactions in the furnace is:

$$2C(s) + O_2(g) \rightarrow 2CO(g) \qquad \Delta H = -221 \, kJ/mol$$

iron ore, coke, limestone

waste gas

hot-air blast

molten slag

molten iron

(a) Name the type of reaction taking place when iron oxide is converted to iron.

.... (1)

(b) Write a balanced symbol equation for the reaction of iron oxide, Fe_2O_3, with carbon monoxide, CO.

.... (2)

(c) Suggest two sources of heat in this process which help to maintain the high temperature inside the furnace.

1 ....

2 .... (2)

(d) Name two gases, other than carbon monoxide, that will be present in the waste gases leaving the furnace.

Gases   .... and .... (1)

(e) Iron from a blast furnace melts at about 1200° C. The melting point of iron is 1500° C. Explain this difference.

.... (1)

(f) Silicon dioxide, SiO_2, is an impurity in iron ore.

Limestone is added to the furnace to convert silicon dioxide into liquid slag.

$$CaCO_3(s) \rightarrow CaO(s) + CO_2(g)$$

$$CaO(s) + SiO_2(s) \rightarrow CaSiO_3(l)$$

$(A_r(Si) = 28, A_r(O) = 16, A_r(Ca) = 40, A_r(C) = 12)$

A 1000 g sample of an ore contained 12% silicon dioxide.

(i) Calculate the mass of silicon dioxide in the 1000 g sample of iron ore.

....g   (1)

(ii) Calculate the number of moles of silicon dioxide in the sample.

(2)

(iii) Calculate the mass of limestone needed to convert the silicon dioxide into slag.

....g   (2)

Quantitative chemistry

Relative atomic mass. A_r This is the number of times the mass of one atom of an element is heavier than the mass of one twelfth of a carbon-12 atom (or approximately the mass of a hydrogen atom).

The mole. A mole is the amount of substance which contains 6×10^{23} particles (Avogadro's number).

1 mole of copper, for example, contains the same number of particles as 1 mole of sulphur atoms and twice as many particles as 0.5 moles of magnesium. The mass of 1 mole of an element or a compound can be found using relative atomic masses.

E.g. mass of 1 mole of   (a) copper, Cu;   (b) oxygen atoms, O;   (c) oxygen molecules, O_2;
                      (d) calcium carbonate, $CaCO_3$;   (e) calcium hydroxide, $Ca(OH)_2$.

(a) $A_r(Cu) = 64$.   Mass of 1 mole of copper atoms $= 64\,g$

(b) $A_r(O) = 16$.   Mass of 1 mole of oxygen atoms $= 16\,g$

(c) Mass of 1 mole of oxygen *molecules* $= 32\,g$

(d) $A_r(Ca) = 40$, $A_r(C) = 12$, $A_r(O) = 16$.
    Mass of 1 mole of calcium carbonate $= 40 + 12 + (3 \times 16) = 100\,g$

(e) $A_r(Ca) = 40$, $A_r(O) = 16$, $A_r(H) = 1$.
    Mass of 1 mole of calcium hydroxide $= 40 + 2(16 + 1) = 74\,g$

You can calculate the number of moles of a substance by dividing the mass of the substance by the mass of 1 mole.

Molar volume

One mole of molecules of any gas occupies a volume of $24\,dm^3$ at room temperature and atmospheric pressure.

Molar solution

A solution containing 1 mole of solute dissolved to make $1\,dm^3$ of solution is called a molar solution (M solution). A 2M solution contains 2 moles of solute in each cubic decimetre of solution.

Empirical formula

This is the simplest formula of a compound in which the atoms are in the correct ratio. CH_2 is the empirical formula for C_2H_4, C_3H_6, C_4H_8, etc. To get the molecular formula it is necessary to know the mass of 1 mole (or relative molecular mass).

The formula of a compound can be obtained from the reacting masses of the reactants.
For example: $6.0\,g$ of carbon combines with $1.0\,g$ of hydrogen.
  Converting into numbers of moles:

        6.0/12 moles of carbon atoms combines with 1.0/1 moles of hydrogen atoms.
        0.5 moles of carbon atoms combines with 1 mole of hydrogen atoms.
        Empirical formula is CH_2.
        If the mass of 1 mole is $28\,g$, the molecular formula is C_2H_4.

The formula of a compound can be obtained in a similar way from percentages. If you are told that a compound of only iron, sulphur and oxygen contains 28% iron and 24% sulphur, you could work out the percentage of oxygen by difference. It is the same as the previous calculation, but using $28\,g$ Fe, $24\,g$ S, and $48\,g$ O.

The percentage of an element present in a compound can be found from the mass of the element present and the mass of 1 mole of the compound. For example, the percentage of nitrogen in ammonium nitrate, NH_4NO_3, can be found if we know that $A_r(N) = 14$, $A_r(H) = 1$, $A_r(O) = 16$.

REVISION SUMMARY

If you need to revise this subject more thoroughly, see the relevant topics in the *Letts* GCSE *Science Study Guide* or *CD-ROM*.

Mass of 1 mole of ammonium nitrate $= 14 + 4 + 14 + (3 \times 16) = 80\,g$
Mass of nitrogen present $= 2 \times 14\,g$
Percentage of nitrogen $= 100 \times 28/80 = 35\%$

Balanced symbolic equations can be used for calculating the quantities of reacting substances and products.

$$E.g. \; CaCO_3 \; + \; 2HCl \; \rightarrow \; CaCl_2 \; + \; H_2O \; + \; CO_2$$

The equation tells us that 1 mole of calcium carbonate (100 g) combines with 2 moles of hydrochloric acid (71 g or $2\,dm^3$ of M solution) to form 1 mole of calcium chloride (111 g) and 1 mole of water (18 g) and 1 mole of carbon dioxide (44 g). Note the sum of the masses of the reactants always equals the sum of the masses of the products.

1 0.327g of the metal X reacted with steam to form 0.407g of the oxide of X.

(a) Calculate the mass of oxygen which reacts with 0.327g of metal X.

.... (1)

(b) Calculate the simplest formula of the oxide of X.

$(A_r(X) = 65.4, A_r(O) = 16)$

(3)

2 Powdered **W** was found to react with water over a few days.
The equation is:

$$W(s) + H_2O(l) \rightarrow WO(s) + H_2(g)$$

0.48g of powdered W was reacted with cold water.
The number of moles of hydrogen molecules formed was calculated each day.
The results are shown in the table.

time days	1	2	3	4	5	6	7
moles of hydrogen	0.006	0.012	0.016	0.019	0.0195	0.020	0.020

After seven days all the metal had reacted.

(a) Plot these results on graph paper. Draw a line of best fit. (3)

(b) How many moles of hydrogen molecules were produced by the complete reaction of W with water?

.... (1)

(c) How many moles of W have reacted in this experiment?

.... (1)

(d) Calculate the mass of one mole of the metal W.

(2)

3 The flow chart below shows the main stages in the production of ammonium nitrate.

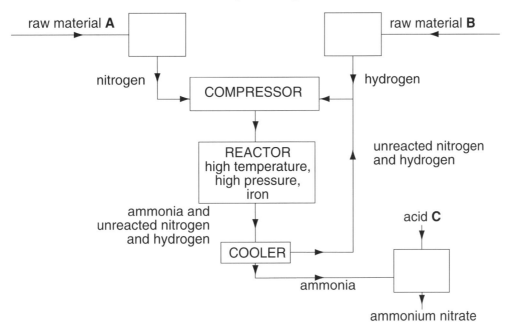

(a) (i) Name the **two** raw materials shown in the flow chart as **A** and **B**.

Raw material **A** ....

Raw material **B** .... (2)

(ii) What is the purpose of the iron in the reactor?

....

.... (1)

(b) (i) Balance the equation which represents the reaction which produces ammonia in the Haber process.

N_2 + ... H_2 $\rightleftharpoons$ .... NH_3 and heat (1)

(ii) The table shows how temperature and pressure affect the amount of ammonia produced in this reaction.

Temperature (°C)	Pressure (atm)	Percentage of nitrogen and hydrogen converted to ammonia (%)
250	200	75
250	1000	96
1000	1	0.01
1000	1000	1

Explain, as fully as you can, why a temperature of about 450°C and a pressure of about 200 atmospheres are normally used in the industrial process.

....

....

....

....

....

....

....

....

....

.... (6)

(c) Look at the flow chart again. Give the name of acid **C** which is added to the ammonia to make ammonium nitrate.

.... (1)

(d) (i) Explain why farmers add ammonium nitrate to the soil.

....

....

.... (2)

(ii) Explain how ammonium nitrate can cause pollution.

....

....

.... (2)

NEAB 1998

The Periodic Table is an arrangement of chemical elements in order of increasing atomic number. Elements with similar properties are in the same vertical column (or group). The horizontal rows are called **periods**.

The Periodic Table was first devised by the Russian chemist Mendeleef in 1869. The Periodic Table below is based upon his original table but elements have been added when they have been discovered. You will have a copy of this table in your examination to help you. Use this table to check the spelling of the element name, the symbol, the mass number, the atomic number and elements with similar properties. For example, if you wish to know about the chemistry of silicon, you will notice it is in the same group as carbon and this should help you write the formula of its oxide as SiO_2, similar to CO_2.

The table consists of eight groups of elements in the **main block**. These are Groups I to VII and 0.

Group I elements are called the alkali metals and Group VII elements are called the halogens. You need to know the chemistry of these two groups. Group O elements are called the noble gases. Between the two parts of the main block are the elements called **transition metals**. These include iron, nickel and copper.

Metals are on the left hand side of the table and non-metals on the right. There is often a bold stepped line to divide metals from non metals. Elements which are gases at room temperature and atmospheric pressure, are in the top right hand corner of the table.

Elements with similar chemical properties, i.e. in the same group, have similar outer electron arrangements, e.g. lithium 2,1 and sodium 2,8,1. Apart from the noble gases, the number of electrons in the outer energy level of any element in the main group is the same as the group number of the element.

REVISION SUMMARY

If you need to revise this subject more thoroughly, see the relevant topics in the _Letts_ GCSE Science Study Guide or CD-ROM.

The Periodic Table of elements

QUESTIONS **1** (a) The chart shows the densities of the first eighteen elements in the Periodic Table (hydrogen to argon).

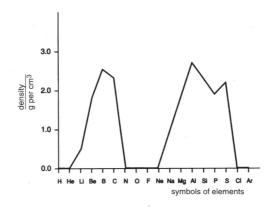

    (i) What does this suggest about the atoms in the two elements at the highest peaks of the chart?

    .... (1)

    (ii) Which Group of the Periodic Table contains these two elements?

    .... (1)

(b) The chart below shows the number of electrons in the outer shell for each of the first eleven elements of the Periodic Table (hydrogen - sodium).

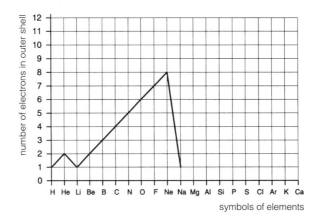

    (i) What is the name given to the family of elements which contains the two elements on the peaks of this chart?

    .... (1)

    (ii) Finish the chart for the elements from sodium to calcium. (2)

(c) The chart on the next page shows the number of electrons in the outer shell for each of the elements of the Periodic Table from scandium to krypton.

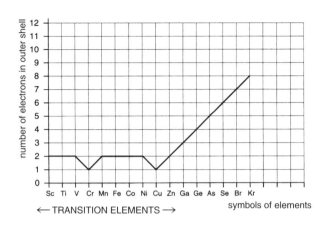

← TRANSITION ELEMENTS →   symbols of elements

Some information about the atomic numbers and atomic radii of the transition metals and the alkali metals (Group I) is given in the tables.

transition metals

element	Sc	Ti	V	Cr	Mn	Fe	Co	Ni	Cu	Zn
atomic number	21	22	23	24	25	26	27	28	29	30
atomic radii/pm	160	146	131	125	112	123	125	124	128	133

alkali metals

element	Li	Na	K	Rb	Cs
atomic number	3	11	19	37	55
atomic radii / pm	152	185	231	246	262

(i) Cobalt and nickel are both transition metals. Why are the properties of cobalt and nickel similar?

....

.... (2)

(ii) Explain why the alkali metals increase in reactivity with increasing atomic number.

....

.... (2)

(iii) Suggest why potassium is more reactive than copper.

....

....

.... (3)

MEG 1997

REVISION SUMMARY

Some chemical reactions are finished in a tiny fraction of a second and some can take millions of years. A reaction which takes place in a very short period of time is called a **fast** reaction. One which takes place over a long period of time is called a **slow** reaction.

The burning of a mixture of hydrogen and oxygen with a squeaky pop is a very fast reaction. The rusting of a steel fence is much slower and the reactions turning vegetable matter into crude oil much slower still. The rate of a chemical reaction can be changed by changing the conditions of the reaction. The souring of milk can be slowed by cooling the milk in a refrigerator.

Factors which speed up a chemical reaction include:

❶ Increasing temperature. As an approximation, in many chemical reactions, a 10°C temperature rise, doubles the rate of reaction.

❷ Increasing the concentration of one or more of the reactants. In the reaction of sodium thiosulphate and dilute hydrochloric acid, doubling the concentration of sodium thiosulphate doubles the rate of the reaction. You must be careful as this relationship, of doubling the rate of a reactant, doubling the rate of the reaction, is not true in all cases.

❸ Using a catalyst. A catalyst alters the rate of a chemical reaction without being used up. Usually a catalyst speeds up a reaction. Some catalysts, called negative catalysts or inhibitors, slow down reactions. A common example of a catalyst is manganese(IV) oxide in the decomposition of hydrogen peroxide into water and oxygen.

❹ Using one of the reactants in a more finely powdered form. For example, powdered calcium carbonate reacts much faster with dilute hydrochloric acid than a lump of calcium carbonate of the same mass.

❺ Using light. A mixture of hydrogen and chlorine explodes in sunlight but does not in the dark. Light can provide the initial energy needed to start a reaction. This is called the **activation energy**.

❻ Increasing pressure. This can increase the speed of a reaction involving gases.

Explaining rate of reaction in a simple particle theory.

You should be able to explain changes in the rate of a chemical reaction in terms of numbers of successful collisions of reacting particles. Increasing the temperature of a reaction mixture speeds up the particles and results in more collisions between particles. It will also result in more collisions where the particles have sufficient energy to react and so the reaction is speeded up.

Increasing the concentration will again result in more particle collisions and therefore the reaction is faster.

A catalyst provides an alternative route for the reaction which needs a lower activation energy. More collisions have this lower energy and so the reaction is faster.

When one of the reactants is powdered, a large surface area is provided. There are therefore more collisions and, as a result, more successful collisions.

Light works in a similar way to heating, by providing additional energy and increasing the pressure is the same as increasing the concentration.

Enzymes

Enzymes are **biological** catalysts which control important processes such as fermentation. An enzyme is a protein. Enzymes work only with certain reactions and under certain conditions. For example, catalase will catalyse the decomposition of hydrogen peroxide but at high temperatures the structure of the enzyme is permanently changed (denatured) and it will no longer work.

If you need to revise this subject more thoroughly, see the relevant topics in the *Letts* GCSE Science Study Guide or CD-ROM.

Letts

1 (a) Indigestion tablets called antacids can be taken to react with excess hydrochloric acid in the stomach. A student investigated two different antacid tablets labelled **X** and **Y**.

   (i) Both tablets, **X** and **Y**, contained calcium carbonate.
       Give the chemical symbol for each of the three elements in calcium carbonate.

       ....

       .... (3)

   (ii) Name the gas formed when calcium carbonate reacts with hydrochloric acid.

       .... (1)

(b) The student first reacted tablet **X** and then tablet **Y**, with 100 cm³ of a hydrochloric acid solution. The student measured the volume of gas produced during the first five minutes. The results are shown in the table.

Time in minutes	0	1	2	3	4	5
Volume of gas in cm³ **Tablet X**	0	38	48	48	48	48
Volume of gas in cm³ **Tablet Y**	0	31	54	67	72	72

   (i) Draw a graph of the results for tablet **Y**.
       (A graph of the results for tablet **X** has been drawn for you.)

       Tablet X

       (3)

   (ii) Tablet **X** contains less calcium carbonate than tablet **Y**.
        How do the results show this?

       .... (1)

   (iii) Explain why the rate of reaction slows down for both tablets.

       ....

       .... (2)

2 2g of small pieces of zinc were put into a beaker. An excess of dilute hydrochloric acid at 20 °C was added and the rate of formation of hydrogen was measured.
The equation for the reaction is given below

$$Zn + 2HCl \rightarrow ZnCl_2 + H_2$$

(a) The rate of formation of hydrogen may be altered if the conditions are changed.

Complete the table stating whether the rate would increase, decrease or remain the same, giving a reason for each answer.

conditions	change in rate	reason
use 2 g of powdered zinc at 20 °C		
use 2 g of the small pieces of zinc at 40 °C		
use 3 g of the small pieces of zinc at 20 °C		

(3)

(b) How will the reaction rate change if 2g of small pieces of magnesium are used instead of zinc? Give a reason for your answer.

change ....

reason .... (2)

(c) In another experiment, 0.5 g of copper powder was added as a catalyst to speed up the reaction between the zinc and the acid. How much copper would remain when the reaction was complete? Give a reason for your answer.

mass of copper left ....

reason ....

.... (2)

(d) Name the salts formed when zinc reacts with

(i) sulphuric acid, ...

(ii) nitric acid. .... (2)

The electron is a fundamental, negatively charged particle that orbits an atomic nucleus. Whenever two objects rub against each other, some electrons are transferred from one to the other. If one of the objects is an insulator, this can lead to a build up of **static charge**. High voltages due to static charge can cause sparks and electric shocks; these are avoided by connecting surfaces to earth. Static charges can be used to clean up the emissions from chimneys; charged smoke particles are **attracted** to a metal plate with the opposite charge and **repelled** from a metal plate with a similar charge.

Movement of charge creates an **electric current**. Electric current is used to transfer energy from the mains supply or a battery to the components in a circuit. The current in a metal is due to movement of electrons; that in a conducting gas or electrolyte is due to the movement of both positively and negatively charged particles.

Current is measured in **amps** (A) using an **ammeter**. In a **series** circuit there is only one current path so the ammeter gives the same reading wherever it is placed. A **parallel** circuit has two or more current paths; depending on where the ammeter is placed, it can be used to measure the current in a single path or the total current in two or more paths. Ammeters are always placed in series with other components, so that all the current being measured passes in them. **Voltmeters**, used to measure **voltage**, are always placed in parallel to measure the voltage across a component.

The amount of electric current passing in a circuit depends on the voltage and the **resistance** in the circuit. Increasing the voltage applies a bigger force to the moving charges, giving a faster flow. Resistance is the opposition to the electric current; more resistance in the circuit reduces the current passing.

The formula for calculating resistance is:

$$\text{resistance} = \frac{\text{voltage}}{\text{current}} \qquad \text{or in symbols} \qquad R = \frac{V}{I}$$

Resistance is measured in **ohms** (symbol Ω).

A metal wire whose temperature does not change has a constant resistance, but the resistance of a lamp filament is much greater when the filament is hot than when it is cold. **Thermistors** have less resistance when warm than when cold and the resistance of a **light dependent resistor** (LDR) depends on its illumination; the brighter the light, the less the resistance.

Diodes only allow a current to pass in one direction (shown by an arrow on the circuit symbol), and even then they only conduct when the voltage rises above a threshold value. Once a diode is conducting, its resistance decreases with increasing current.

Voltage is a measure of the energy transfer in a component or circuit. A 12 V power supply transfers 12 joules of energy to each coulomb of charge. When the charge flows through a lamp the energy is transferred into heat and light. Voltage measures energy transfer both ways – the voltage across a power supply measures the energy transfer to the charge and the voltage across a component measures the energy transfer **from** the charge.

Power measures the energy transferred each second; this is determined by both the current and the voltage.

The following equations show the relationships between current, charge, power and voltage.

$$\text{current (in A)} = \frac{\text{charge flow (in C)}}{\text{time (in s)}} \qquad I = \frac{Q}{t}$$

$$\text{voltage (in V)} = \frac{\text{energy transfer (in J)}}{\text{charge (in C)}} \qquad V = \frac{E}{Q}$$

$$\text{power (in W)} = \text{current (in A)} \times \text{voltage (in V)} \quad P = IV$$

REVISION SUMMARY

Electric current from a battery is **direct current** (d.c.) but that from the mains is **alternating current** (a.c.). Charge flow that forms a direct current is always in the same direction but the flow changes direction in an alternating current.

The domestic electricity supply uses alternating current. Energy is supplied through the live wire, the neutral wire being the return path for the current. The **earth** wire is connected to the ground and is for safety.

Electric appliances need to be fitted with safety features to reduce the risk of fire and electrocution. **Fuses** or **circuit breakers** fitted in the consumer unit should cut off the current if it reaches such a level that the wiring cables are in danger of overheating and setting on fire. In a similar way, fuses fitted to plugs protect from fire hazard. The fuse wire melts and this stops the current if there is a fault that causes a larger than normal current to pass.

Earth wires should be connected to the casing of any appliance that has a metal case. Should the case become "live" a large current then passes to earth which melts the fuse and cuts off the electrical supply.

The **joule** is too small a unit for measuring the energy supplied to homes so the electricity supply industry uses the **kilowatt hour**. The energy transferred is calculated using the formula:

$$\text{energy (in kWh)} = \text{power (in kW)} \times \text{time (in h)}$$

Magnets have **poles**, the strongest parts of the magnet, usually along the faces or at the ends of a bar magnet. Like poles repel each other and unlike poles attract. The **magnetic field** around a magnet is the name given to the region where it exerts forces on magnetic materials; the direction of the field at any point is the direction of the force it exerts on the north-seeking pole of a magnet.

Electric currents also have magnetic fields; a current-carrying wire placed at right angles to the field between two attracting magnets experiences a force that is at right angles to both the current in the wire and the magnetic field direction. This is used in devices such as relays, motors and loudspeakers to produce movement.

Electromagnetic induction is the name given to the way in which electricity is generated and transformed. In a generator or bicycle dynamo a magnet rotates inside a coil of wire. The changing magnetic field causes a voltage to be induced; the size of the **induced voltage** depends on the **rate** at which the magnetic field changes.

Transformers are efficient devices which use electromagnetism for changing the size of an alternating voltage. The equation for this is:

If you need to revise this subject more thoroughly, see the relevant topics in the *Letts* **GCSE Science Study Guide or CD-ROM.**

$$\frac{\text{number of turns on primary coil}}{\text{number of turns on secondary coil}} = \frac{\text{primary voltage}}{\text{secondary voltage}} \qquad \frac{N_p}{N_s} = \frac{V_p}{V_s}$$

Transformers do not give a free supply of energy; when used to increase the voltage they reduce the current and they give increased currents when the voltage is reduced.

$$\frac{\text{number of turns on primary coil}}{\text{number of turns on secondary coil}} = \frac{\text{secondary current}}{\text{primary current}} \qquad \frac{N_p}{N_s} = \frac{I_s}{I_p}$$

The electricity supply industry makes extensive use of transformers; transmitting energy at high voltages enables low currents to be used which reduces the energy losses in transmission. Transformers **step up** the voltage at the power station before the energy is fed into the grid and **step down** the voltage in several stages before the energy is delivered to homes, commerce and industry.

1 When a car is being filled with petrol, the petrol can become negatively charged as it flows down the metal pipe to the petrol tank.

(a) Explain how the petrol becomes negatively charged.

....

.... (2)

(b) What type of charge does the metal pipe gain?

.... (1)

(c) The presence of a person's hand near the metal pipe can cause an explosion.
Suggest how this can occur.

....

....

.... (3)

(d) There is no risk of an explosion if the metal pipe is connected to the bodywork of the car.
Explain how this prevents an explosion.

....

.... (2)

2 (a) The table below shows the current in three different electrical appliances when
connected to the 240 V mains a.c. supply.

Appliance	Current in A
kettle	8.5
lamp	0.4
toaster	4.8

(i) Which appliance has the greatest electrical resistance?

....

How does the data show this?

....

.... (2)

(ii) The lamp is connected to the mains supply using thin, twin-cored cable, consisting of live and neutral connections.
State **two** reasons why this cable should not be used for connecting the kettle to the mains supply.

1 ....

2 .... (2)

(b) (i) Calculate the power rating of the kettle when it is operated from the 240 V a.c. mains supply.

(3)

(ii) A holiday-maker takes the kettle abroad where the mains supply is 120 V. What is the current in the kettle when it is operated from the 120 V supply? You can assume that the resistance of the kettle does not change.

.... (1)

(iii) The kettle is filled with water. Explain how the time it takes to boil the kettle changes when it is operated from the 120 V supply.

....

.... (2)

Edexcel 1998

3 Electricity retailers sell energy to domestic customers in units of kWh.
The cost of each kWh is around 7p.

In a household, a 2.5 kW immersion heater is in use for 1.5 hours each day.

(a) Calculate the energy transfer and the cost of that energy in a 90-day period.

....

....

.... (3)

(b) The heater is accidentally left switched on overnight, for a period of 12 hours. Explain why the energy transfer to the heater in this time is much less than 30 kWh.

....

.... (2)

(c) There are three conductors in the cable to the heater. These are called earth, live and neutral.

(i) Describe the function of the live and neutral conductors.

....

.... (2)

(ii) Explain how the earth wire, along with the fuse, prevents the user from electrocution.

....

....

.... (3)

4 The diagram shows a circuit used to investigate the resistance of a carbon rod.

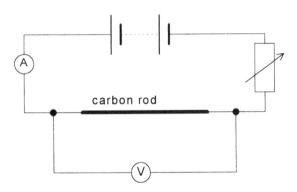

(a) Write down **two** ways of changing the current in the circuit.

....

.... (2)

(b) The table shows the ammeter and voltmeter readings for a range of current passing in the rod.

voltage V	current A
0.8	0.4
1.9	1.1
3.1	2.1
4.1	3.2
4.7	4.1

(i) Use squared paper to plot a graph of voltage against current. (3)

(ii) Read from your graph the value of the voltage when the current in the carbon rod is 1.5 A.

.... (1)

(iii) Calculate the resistance of the carbon rod when the current in it is 1.5 A.

....

....

.... (3)

5 Many radios can work from either batteries or the mains electricity supply. A transformer is used to convert the mains voltage to the value needed by the radio. The transformer can be built into either the radio or the mains plug.

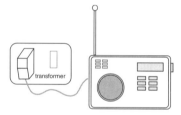

One radio has the following label printed on it.

Supply into transformer	240V	0.01A
Output from transformer	6V	0.35A
Battery operation	6V	0.3A

(a) (i) Give the formula that links the power of an electrical device, the voltage and the current.

.... (1)

(ii) Calculate the power when the radio is working from batteries.

....watts (2)

The transformer that is used to convert the mains voltage is made of two coils of wire wrapped around a soft iron core.

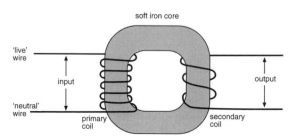

(b) Explain why a transformer will produce an output voltage when an a.c. supply is connected to the primary coil, but not when a d.c. supply is used.

....

.... (2)

(c) The input voltage to the primary coil is 240V. The output voltage from the secondary coil is 6V. If the primary coil has 8000 turns, how many turns must the secondary coil have?

....

.... (3)

MEG 1995

6 The diagram below shows a coil of wire connected to a meter which can measure small currents.

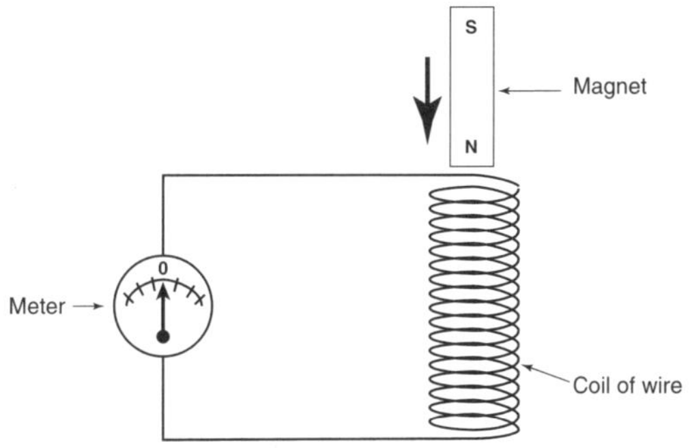

(a) What, if anything, happens to the needle of the meter as the magnet is moved into the coil?

.... (1)

(b) The magnet is now left stationary inside the coil as shown in the diagram below.

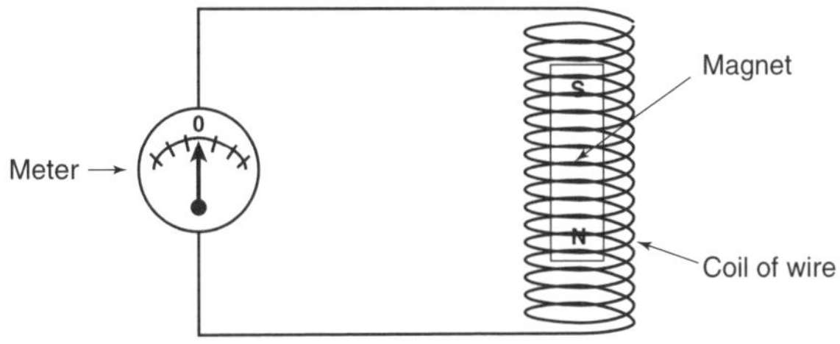

What, if anything, happens to the needle of the meter?

.... (1)

(c) What, if anything, happens to the needle of the meter as the magnet is lifted out of the coil?

....

.... (2)

NEAB 1997

13 Forces and motion

Forces can cause objects to change in size or shape, speed or direction of motion. Whenever one object pulls or pushes another, each object exerts the same size force on the other, but the forces are in opposite directions.

Springs and metal wires follow Hooke's Law when subjected to a stretching force; the extension is proportional to the force up to the limit of proportionality. Materials that return to their original size and shape when a force is removed are said to be elastic. Rubber is elastic, as are metals up to their elastic limit; beyond this they deform permanently. Plasticine and Blu-tack are plastic materials; their shape is easily changed and they retain the new shape when the force is removed.

The **pressure** caused by a force is a measure of how effective it is at piercing or deforming the surface that it acts on. Drawing pins and scissors are designed so that the force exerts a large pressure and penetrates the surface. Skis and caterpillar tracks on vehicles ensure that the force is applied over a large area to reduce the pressure. The formula for calculating pressure is:

$$\text{pressure} = \frac{\text{force}}{\text{area}} \qquad \text{or in symbols} \qquad P = \frac{F}{A}$$

The unit of pressure is the **pascal (Pa)** which is equivalent to a **N/m²**.

In **hydraulic** systems, liquids are used to transmit pressure. Because liquids exert an equal pressure in all directions, the pressure can be easily transmitted round corners. By changing the **area** over which the pressure acts, the **force** can be made bigger or smaller.

Taps, bicycle pedals and doors are common examples of situations where forces are used to turn things round. How effective a force is at causing rotation depends not only on the size of the force, but also on the shortest distance from the line it acts along to the pivot. The **moment**, or **turning effect**, of a force is calculated using the formula:

moment = force × shortest (or perpendicular) distance from force line to pivot

The moment, or turning effect, of a force is measured in **Nm**. In situations where the turning effects of a number of forces cancel out, the object is **balanced** or **in equilibrium**. This is known as the 'law of moments' which states that: When an object is in equilibrium, the sum of the clockwise moments about any pivot is equal to the sum of the anticlockwise moments about that pivot.

Changing the pressure of a gas causes its volume to change. Provided that the amount of gas and its temperature are unchanged, the pressure is inversely proportional to the volume. This means that if one of the quantities is doubled, the other one halves. This is known as **Boyle's law** and can be written as:

pressure × volume = constant or $P_1V_1 = P_2V_2$.

Cars, bikes, buses, trains and other moving objects often have more than one force acting and so the overall effect of all the forces acting has to be taken into account. If the forces acting cancel out there is no effect on the movement of the object; it either stays put or moves in a straight line at a constant speed.

The **average speed** of a moving object is calculated using the equation:

$$\text{average speed} = \frac{\text{distance travelled}}{\text{time taken}} \qquad \text{or in symbols} \qquad v = \frac{s}{t}$$

Speed can also be calculated from a graph of distance travelled against time; the gradient or slope of the graph represents the speed.

Objects moving with the same speed in different directions have different **velocities**. The velocity of an object gives two pieces of information; its speed and direction.

When the forces are not balanced the effect is to change the speed or direction of an object.

This is known as acceleration which is calculated using the formula

$$\text{acceleration} = \frac{\text{increase in velocity}}{\text{time taken}} \quad \text{or in symbols} \quad a = \frac{(v - u)}{t}$$

Acceleration can be thought of as the increase in speed per second and is measured in **m/s^2**.

The acceleration caused by an unbalanced force depends on the mass being accelerated as well as the size of the unbalanced force – a double decker bus needs a much bigger force than a mini car to give it the same acceleration. The equation which relates the mass of the object to the size of the unbalanced force and the acceleration it causes is:

$$\text{force} = \text{mass} \times \text{acceleration} \quad \text{or in symbols} \quad F = ma$$

An object falling freely in the absence of air resistance has an acceleration, g, equal to 10 m/s^2. As an object falling through air or any other fluid speeds up, the resistive force increases. The effect of this is to reduce the size of the unbalanced force and the acceleration. Eventually **terminal velocity** is reached when the downward force, the object's **weight**, is balanced by the resistive force.

The **stopping distance** of a vehicle is the distance it travels between the time when a driver notices a hazard and the vehicle coming to rest. The factors that affect stopping distance include the driver's **reaction time** as well as the speed and mass of the vehicle and the conditions of the road, tyres and brakes.

If you need to revise this subject more thoroughly, see the relevant topics in the *Letts* GCSE *Science Study Guide* or *CD-ROM*.

1   The graph shows how the speed of a cyclist changes on a short journey.

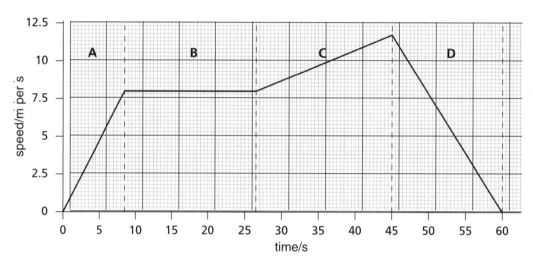

(i)   Describe the motion of the cyclist in each of the sections shown on the graph.

A   ....

B   ....

C   ....

D   .... (4)

(ii) Calculate the distance travelled by the cyclist in the period from 9 s to 26 s, section
      B on the graph.

(3)

(iii) Calculate the acceleration of the cyclist in the first 9 s, section **A** on the graph.

(3)

(iv) Calculate the unbalanced force needed to cause this acceleration if the combined
     mass of the cyclist and the cycle is 95 kg.

(3)

(v) Section A of the graph shows a constant acceleration. Suggest why it is likely in real life that the acceleration of the cyclist decreases as the speed increases.

....

.... (2)

(vi) Calculate the braking force required to stop the cycle and cyclist in section **D** of the graph.

(4)

(vii) Calculate the braking distance in section **D** of the graph. (*Hint: the **average** speed is not 12 m/s.*)

(3)

(viii) Assuming the same braking force is used, calculate the braking distance from a speed of 6 m/s.

(3)

(ix) Explain why the braking distance from a speed of 12 m/s is four times that from a speed of 6 m/s.

....

....

.... (3)

QUESTIONS 2 The diagram shows a hand operated hydraulic jack.

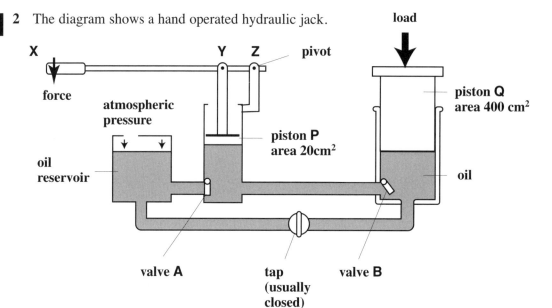

A force is applied downwards at **X** on the lever **XZ**. This causes the piston to move downwards. Valve **A** closes and oil is forced through valve **B** to raise piston **Q**.

When lever **XZ** is lifted again, valve **B** closes and valve **A** opens to allow oil from the reservoir to pass through.

The area of piston **P** is $20\,cm^2$ and that of piston **Q** is $400\,cm^2$.

(a) The downward force exerted by piston **P** on the oil is $200\,N$.

Calculate, in N/cm^2, the pressure applied by piston **P** to the oil.

....

....

.... (2)

(b) What is the pressure under piston **Q**?

.... (1)

(c) Calculate the force exerted by the oil on piston **Q**.

....

.... (2)

(d) Piston **P** moves down by 2 cm.

(i) Calculate the volume of oil moved out of the cylinder below **P**.

....

.... (2)

(ii) Calculate how far piston **Q** rises.

....

.... (2)

(iii) What have you assumed about the oil in the hydraulic jack?

.... (1)

MEG 1996

3 A sky diver jumps out of an aircraft and falls towards the Earth.

(a) What two forces act on the sky diver? State the direction of each force.

....

.... (4)

The graph shows how the speed of the sky diver changes before the parachute is opened.

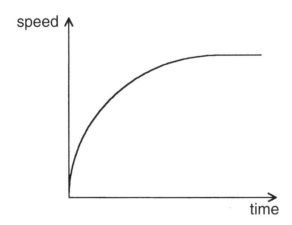

(b) Which part of the graph shows the sky diver travelling at terminal velocity?

.... (1)

(c) Use the graph to describe how the acceleration of the sky diver changes.

....

.... (2)

(d) In terms of the forces acting on the sky diver, explain why the acceleration changes in this way.

....

....

.... (3)

4 Nitrous oxide gas is used as the propellant in some aerosol cans that contain food such as cream. The diagram shows one such can.

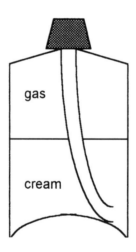

gas

cream

The full aerosol contains $150\,cm^3$ of cream and $175\,cm^3$ of gas at a pressure of $5.0 \times 10^5\,Pa$.

(a) Assuming that no gas escapes, calculate the volume of the gas when all the cream has been squirted out of the aerosol.

.... (1)

(b) Calculate the pressure of the gas when all the cream has been squirted out of the aerosol.

....

....

.... (3)

Waves transfer energy; they are important for communications as well as heating and lighting the space that we live in.

Sound is carried to our ears by a to-and-fro movement of air particles. This to-and-fro movement starts with a **vibrating** object such as a loudspeaker which sets the air particles into a **longitudinal** wave motion where the vibrations are along the direction in which the wave is travelling.

The maximum amount of displacement (movement to one side or the other) of the air particles is called the **amplitude** of the wave; the greater the amplitude, the louder the sound. The graph shows how the movement of an individual air molecule changes with time.

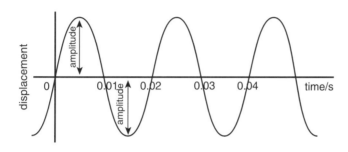

As well as showing the amplitude, the graph has a time scale that enables the **frequency** to be measured. The frequency of a wave is the number of oscillations per second. The sound wave shown on the graph does one complete oscillation in 0.02 or 1/50 second so it has a frequency of 50 waves per second, or 50 hertz (Hz). The frequency of a sound wave determines its pitch; 50 Hz is quite a low-pitched sound but frequencies of 1000 Hz or more are high-pitched.

Measurements of the **wavelength** and **frequency** allow the **speed** of sound to be calculated using the formula:

$$\text{speed} = \text{frequency} \times \text{wavelength} \quad \text{or in symbols} \quad v = f\lambda$$

Reflections of sound or **ultrasound**, a longitudinal wave with a frequency above the range of human hearing, are called echoes. Echoes can be used to measure distances and to scan body organs.

Light is a small part of a family of waves called the **electromagnetic spectrum**. Most objects do not give off light so we rely on reflected light to be able to see them. All but the smoothest of surfaces reflect light in all directions. Mirrors are smooth surfaces that reflect light in a predictable way – the angles of incidence and reflection are equal. The reflection of light by a mirror causes a **virtual image** to be formed. Our eye-brain system assumes that light travels in straight lines so when we look into a mirror the reflected light looks to have come from a point the same distance behind the mirror as the object is in front of it.

Mirrors are not the only things that cause the direction in which light travels to change; light can also change direction when it passes through transparent objects such as glass. The change in speed when light passes from one substance to another is called **refraction**. This causes a change in wavelength and, except when light hits the boundary at a right angle, a change in direction. Although the wavelength and speed both change when light is refracted, the frequency, which determines the colour of the light, remains constant.

Light does not always pass into the new substance when it meets a boundary. Light travelling from glass to air is **totally internally reflected** for angles of incidence greater than 42°. Total internal reflection is used in bicycle reflectors, prism binoculars, cats' eyes and fibre optics.

QUESTIONS The table shows the main parts of the electromagnetic spectrum and their uses.

Wave	gamma rays	X-rays	ultra-violet	visible light	infra-red	microwaves	radio waves
Typical wavelength /m	1×10^{-12}	1×10^{-9}	1×10^{-7}	5×10^{-7}	1×10^{-6}	1×10^{-1}	100
Use	sterilizing medical equipment treating cancers and tumours taking images of body organs	X-ray photographs treating cancers and tumours taking images of body organs	treatment of skin disorders, responsible for suntans	seeing and transmitting data	heating and armchair operation of tv equipment	cooking and transmitting data	broadcasting

The shorter wavelength waves are the most penetrative and also the most ionising so they pose the greatest dangers. Exposure to waves of shorter wavelength than light should be limited.

All electromagnetic waves are **transverse** waves – the vibrations are at right angles to the direction of travel.

All waves spread out when they pass through a narrow opening; this is called **diffraction**. The amount of spreading depends on the size of the opening relative to the wavelength; if the opening is hundreds of wavelengths wide then very little spreading occurs, with maximum spreading when the opening is equal to the wavelength. Sound waves (typical wavelength 1 metre) spread out when passing through a doorway but light waves do not.

Both transverse and longitudinal waves pass through the Earth following an earthquake when layers of rock slip past each other. Longitudinal waves can be detected at all points on the Earth's surface but transverse waves cannot be detected on the side of the Earth opposite to the disturbance. This provides evidence that the outer core is liquid, since liquids transmit longitudinal waves but do not transmit transverse waves.

1 (a) A sound wave travelling through air can be represented as shown in the diagram.

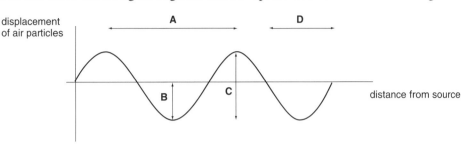

Which distance, **A**, **B**, **C**, or **D** represents:

(i) one wavelength? ....

(ii) the amplitude of the wave?... (2)

(b) The cone of a loudspeaker is vibrating. The diagram shows how the air particles are spread out in front of the cone at a certain time.

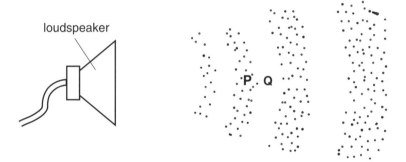

P is a compression, **Q** is a rarefaction.

(i) Describe how the pressure in the air changes from **P** to **Q**.

....

.... (2)

(ii) Describe the motion of the air particles as the sound wave passes.

....

.... (2)

(iii) **On the diagram** of the air particles above, mark and label a distance equal to one wavelength of the sound wave. (1)

MEG 1997

2 (a) Mirrors and flat surfaces of water or glass reflect light in a predictable way. A person standing by a lake can see a tree on the opposite side of the lake and also an image of the tree in the lake.

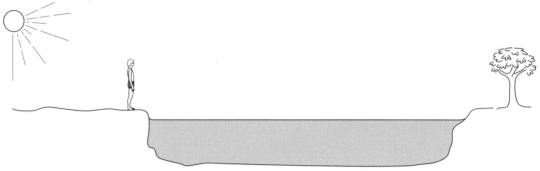

(i) Explain how light from the Sun enables the person to see the tree.

.... (1)

(ii) Draw on the diagram to show how light from the tree can be reflected by the lake to the person's eye.

.... (1)

(iii) Sketch on the diagram the image of the tree that the person sees. (3)

(iv) Is the image a real or a virtual one? Explain how you can tell.

....

.... (2)

(b) Not all of the light is reflected at the water surface; some passes into the water, where it slows down. The diagram below represents wavefronts of light approaching the water surface from two directions.

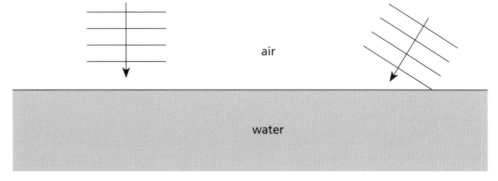

air

water

The speed of light in water is approximately three-quarters of its speed in air. Complete the diagrams to show the wavefronts as they pass through the water. (4)

3 The electromagnetic spectrum is a family of waves with wavelengths ranging from approximately 1×10^{-15} m to hundreds of metres. The waves with shorter wavelengths than visible light are the most hazardous to humans.

(a) Name **two** types of electromagnetic radiation with a wavelength shorter than light.

....

....

.... (2)

(b) For each of the two types of radiation that you named in (a): describe briefly

   (i) the origin of the radiation

   (ii) one use of the radiation

   (iii) one possible danger of the radiation

   (iv) one precaution that should be taken to protect people who come into contact with that radiation.

....

....

....

....

....

....

....

....

....

....

....

.... (8)

REVISION SUMMARY

The **Universe** is everything that exists; it is thought to have begun in an enormous explosion about fifteen billion years ago. Within the Universe there are groups of stars called **galaxies**. Our star is the Sun and our galaxy is the **Milky Way**, which is a whirling spiral, held together by the attractive **gravitational forces** that act between massive objects.

Gravitational forces act between all objects that have mass, with each object pulling the other. The size of the gravitational force between two 1 kg masses such as two bags of sugar is tiny, but the size becomes appreciable when one of the objects is very massive.

Planets move around the Sun in elliptical orbits that are almost circular; they are kept in orbit by the Sun's gravitational pull. Similarly, the orbit of a planetary moon is due to the planet's gravitational pull on the moon.

Although the Earth has only one natural satellite, there are many artificial ones. Like the Moon, they are kept in orbit by the gravitational attraction of the Earth. This gravitational attraction decreases with increasing distance from the Earth.

Stars are formed in large clouds of gas and dust that contract due to gravitational attraction. As they contract they heat until the temperature is hot enough for them to generate energy by **nuclear fusion**. After its **main sequence**, a star cools and expands to a **red supergiant**. Contraction due to gravitational forces causes heating. A small star like our Sun becomes a white dwarf and continues to cool but a large star forms a **blue supergiant**. Further expansion and contraction leads to the formation of a very bright star called a **supernova** which eventually explodes, forming a very dense **neutron star** and a dust cloud. Our Solar System is thought to have formed from the remnants of an exploding supernova.

The core of the dust cloud formed the Sun, with the outermost material condensing to form the planets. In addition to the nine planets, there is the **asteroid belt** and collections of ice and dust known as **comets**. Comets can have very long orbit times, often hundreds of years.

The inner planets, Mercury, Venus, Earth and Mars, are the denser ones in the Solar System; they have a high concentration of metals. Beyond the asteroid belt, Jupiter and Saturn are composed largely of hydrogen and helium. Little is known about the composition of the three outermost planets. Uranus and Neptune are thought to have a rocky core surrounded by a liquid mantle and an atmosphere of hydrogen and helium. Pluto is also thought to be rocky, with a surface of frozen methane.

The Universe is still expanding, as it has been doing since its formation. The rate of expansion is measured from **red shift**, the shifting of the wavelength of the light emitted by a star towards the red end of the spectrum. When the paths of the galaxies are plotted, all these paths trace back to the same point. This is thought to be the point where the Universe was created. The age of the Universe is estimated by measuring the speed at which the galaxies are moving away from each other and extrapolating back to the beginning of time.

There are three possibilities for the future of the Universe. It may carry on expanding for ever or the gravitational forces may slow down the expansion and eventually cause it to contract again with catastrophic results. The third model is that the gravitational forces are not strong enough to cause a collapse but are just strong enough to prevent continued expansion, so the Universe will eventually reach a stable size.

If you need to revise this subject more thoroughly, see the relevant topics in the *Letts* GCSE *Science Study Guide* or CD-ROM.

1 (a) Jupiter is the largest planet in the Solar System. It is thought to consist mainly of hydrogen and helium.
Explain why the density of Jupiter is less than that of the Earth.

....

.... (2)

(b) The table below compares some features of Jupiter and Earth.

Feature	Earth	Jupiter
average surface temperature in °C	20	−120
magnetic field	strong	very strong
density in g/cm³	5.5	1.3
time to rotate on axis in hours	24	10
time to orbit Sun in years	1	11.9
mean orbital speed in millions of km/hour	0.11	0.05
surface gravitational field strength in N/kg	10	23

(i) Which feature suggests that the core of Jupiter contains iron?

.... (1)

(ii) Explain why Jupiter takes much longer than the Earth to orbit the Sun.

....

....

.... (3)

(iii) Suggest why the temperature at the surface of Jupiter is less than that at the surface of the Earth.

....

....

.... (2)

(c) Jupiter has several moons. One of them, Io, is about the size of the Earth's moon.
There is volcanic activity on Io. Conditions on Io differ from those on the Earth's moon.
Suggest **two** differences.

1 ....

2 .... (2)

QUESTIONS

(d) A probe entered Jupiter's atmosphere.
The probe was fitted with a parachute to reduce its speed as it entered the atmosphere.
The probe sent back information about the atmosphere for over an hour before it was destroyed.

(i) Suggest why the probe was destroyed as it fell through the atmosphere.

....

.... (1)

(ii) Explain how the parachute prolonged the 'life' of the probe as it fell.

....

....

.... (2)

Edexcel 1998

2 The universe is thought to have started with an enormous explosion. The first substances that formed after the explosion were hydrogen and helium. Heavier elements were later formed in stars.

(a) Suggest how the heavier elements could have formed.

....

.... (2)

(b) Explain why our solar system could not have been formed at the same time as the first stars in the universe.

....

.... (2)

(c) One theory about the origin of the solar system is that it was formed from a spinning cloud of dust that was part of the remains of an exploding supernova. Explain how this theory explains the fact that the innermost planets are denser than the outer planets.

....

.... (2)

(d) The universe is still expanding, but the rate of expansion is decreasing. Suggest why the rate of expansion is decreasing.

....

.... (2)

(e) Explain how the expansion of the universe supports the theory that it started as a single explosion.

....

.... (2)

3   The table shows the period of orbit for Earth satellites which have different radii of orbit.

radius of orbit 1000 km	period of orbit 1000 s
10	10
20	28
30	50
40	78

(a) Use squared paper to plot a graph of period of orbit against radius of orbit. The period of orbit axis should extend to 90 000 s and the radius of orbit axis to 50 000 km. (3)

(b) Describe how the period of orbit varies with radius of orbit.

.... (1)

(c) (i)   What is the radius of orbit for a satellite with a period of orbit of 24 hours? Explain how you arrived at your answer.

....

.... (2)

(ii) State and explain a use for such a satellite.

....

.... (2)

(d) How does the speed of an orbiting satellite vary with the radius of its orbit? Explain how you arrived at your answer.

....

.... (2)

Edexcel 1996

16 Energy resources and energy transfer

Nothing can happen without an energy transfer. A braking car is transferring **kinetic** energy into **thermal** energy or **heat**; when it accelerates **chemical** energy from the fuel is being transferred into kinetic energy, but a car travelling at a constant speed on the level is just transferring chemical energy into thermal energy of the surroundings!

Devices such as heaters, lamps, television sets and radios are designed to carry out a particular energy transfer; a gas fire is designed to transfer chemical energy from the gas into thermal energy and a lamp is designed to transfer energy from electricity into light. Although all the energy that goes into one of these devices must come out (this is known as conservation of energy; the total amount of energy remains the same), it does not all come out in the desired form.

Tungsten filament lamps are poor at achieving the desired energy transfer, typically producing about 5 J of light for every 100 J energy supplied from electricity.

Modern fluorescent lamps are more efficient; they transfer more of the energy input into the desired output, ie light. The efficiency of a device is the fraction or percentage of the energy input that is output in a useful form. Filament lamps have an efficiency of about 5% while that for fluorescent lamps is about 20%.

There are four mechanisms by which energy from hot objects such as lamps and heaters is lost to the surroundings. Everything emits **infra-red radiation**; the rate of emission increases with increasing temperature and also depends on the nature of the surface. A dull, dark surface emits more radiation than a shiny one at the same temperature. The dark surface is also a better absorber than the shiny one; aluminium foil and silvered surfaces are used as insulators because they reflect infra-red radiation so they can reduce the amount leaving a hot object or entering a cold one.

A second mechanism is by **conduction**; the transfer of energy from an energetic molecule to a less energetic one when they collide. Conduction in metals is a more rapid process than in non-metals because the free electrons diffuse within the metal, spreading the energy around. Gases are poor conductors of thermal energy because of the relatively large spacing between the particles compared to a liquid or a solid.

The third mechanism is by **convection currents**, which only occur in fluids; they are caused by differences in density when part of the fluid is warmed or cooled. Convection currents keep the air circulating in a refrigerator and in a room that is heated by a 'radiator'.

Liquids and objects that contain moisture can also lose energy by **evaporation**. When this happens the more energetic particles leave the surface of the liquid, so the average energy of the particles remaining in the liquid is reduced, causing the liquid to cool.

Insulation is most effective when it targets the main form of energy transfer. Warm objects such as people and their houses lose most energy by conduction and convection. They can be insulated by trapping layers of air in such things as clothing and cavity wall insulation. Air is a poor conductor, but it needs to be trapped to stop energy transfer by convection currents.

Hot moist objects such as food taken from an oven lose most energy by radiation and evaporation. Covering food with aluminium foil is an effective way of keeping it warm for short periods of time.

Most of the energy that we transfer in our homes comes from fossil fuels; energy from the Sun was trapped millions of years ago and stored as **chemical** energy. Fossil fuels are **non-renewable**; we cannot make any more coal, gas or oil. Nuclear fission fuels such as uranium are also non-renewable. Some electricity is generated from renewable sources; **hydroelectric power** uses energy from the Sun that drives the water cycle and **wind** power uses energy from the Sun that causes movement of airstreams. Solar cells transfer energy from the Sun directly into electricity but their high cost and low efficiency give them limited use in the UK.

Our bodies use **renewable** energy sources; plants transfer energy from the Sun into chemical energy or **biomass**; unlike the formation of coal, this is a short-term process and one that can be repeated many times in a short timescale.

Cost is an important factor when choosing an energy source and this is often governed by availability. Environmental factors are increasingly being taken into account but whereas wind 'farms' do not cause the atmospheric pollution associated with fossil fuels, some people regard them as being noisy and ugly. Social factors to be taken into account include employment and environmental changes that could affect tourism or the livelihood of a community.

Forces that cause movement are doing work and transferring energy. The amount of work done or energy transferred is calculated using the formula:

$$\text{work done} = \text{force} \times \text{distance moved in direction of force}$$
$$\text{or in symbols} \quad W = fd$$

Work and energy are measured in **joules** (J).

The rate at which work is done or energy is transferred is called the **power**; this is the work done by a force each second and is measured in **watts** (W). Power is calculated using the formula:

$$\text{power} = \frac{\text{work done/energy transfer}}{\text{time taken}} \quad \text{or in symbols} \quad P = \frac{E}{t}$$

Using a force to lift an object vertically is an example of transferring energy to **gravitational potential energy** (gpe for short). The gravitational potential energy gained by the object is calculated using the formula:

$$\text{change in gpe} = \text{weight} \times \text{change in height} \quad \text{or in symbols} \quad gpe = mg\Delta h$$

The symbol g stands for the gravitational field strength which is the weight of each kg of material. The gravitational field strength at the surface of the Earth is about 10 N/kg and that at the surface of the Moon is about 1.5 N/kg.

When an object changes speed its **kinetic energy** (ke) changes. The formula for kinetic energy is:

$$\text{kinetic energy} = \tfrac{1}{2} \times \text{mass} \times (\text{velocity})^2 \quad \text{or in symbols} \quad ke = \tfrac{1}{2}mv^2$$

For an object moving vertically in the absence of air resistance, the energy transfer is between gravitational potential energy and kinetic energy, so the change in gpe is equal to the change in ke.

If you need to revise this subject more thoroughly, see the relevant topics in the *Letts* GCSE *Science Study Guide* or CD-ROM.

1 When an electric kettle is heating water, energy is being transferred to the water and to the surroundings. The diagram illustrates three ways in which energy is transferred to the surroundings.

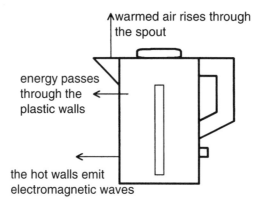

(a) For each of these energy transfers, write down the word from the list which describes it.

conduction   convection   radiation

You may use each word once, more than once or not at all.

(i) Warmed air rises through the spout.   ....   (1)

(ii) Energy passes through the plastic walls.   ....   (1)

(iii) The hot walls emit electromagnetic waves.   ....   (1)

(b) (i) Describe, in terms of the motion of particles, how energy is transferred through the kettle walls.

....

....

....   (3)

(ii) Some kettles are double-walled. The diagram shows how a layer of air is trapped between the inner wall and the outer wall.

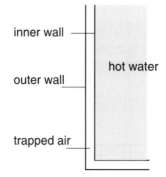

Suggest **one** advantage of using a double-walled kettle.

....

.... (1)

MEG 1996

2 Although most of the electricity generated in the UK comes from burning fossil fuels such as coal, oil and gas, a significant amount is generated using moving water; this is called 'hydroelectric power'.

(a) Write down **three** advantages of using hydroelectric power instead of burning fossil fuels.

....

....

.... (3)

(b) What is the energy source for hydroelectric power ?

.... (1)

(c) In a pumped storage system, water is pumped from a low reservoir to a high one at night when there is little demand for electricity. The water can be released, generating electricity as it goes back to the low reservoir, in order to satisfy peak demand. The diagram shows the arrangement of the reservoirs.

Water released to generate electricity at peak demand

Water pumped to high level reservoir at night using surplus electricity

Turbines and pumps/generators

(i) Describe the energy transfer when the station is generating electricity.

....

....

.... (3)

(ii) In a pumped storage station, the maximum water flow downhill is 2.5×10^5 kg each second. This water falls through a height of 190 m. Calculate the energy lost by 2.5×10^5 kg of water in falling through a height of 190 m.

(3)

(iii) The energy from the water is transferred to electricity with an efficiency of 60%. Use the formula

$$\text{efficiency} = \frac{\text{useful power output}}{\text{total power input}}$$

to calculate the maximum power output of the station.

(3)

(iv) Suggest **one** factor that limits the efficiency of a pumped storage station when it is generating electricity.

....

....

.... (2)

(v) Pumped storage stations do not produce electricity. It takes more electrical energy to pump the water uphill than is recovered when it moves down. Suggest **two** advantages of using pumped storage rather than building more power stations to satisfy peak demand.

....

.... (2)

3 As an alternative to lifting a heavy load onto the back of a lorry, a ramp can be used to pull it up a slope.

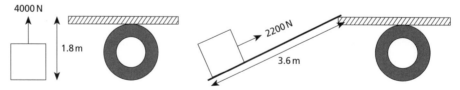

(a) Calculate the work done when the load is lifted onto the lorry.

(3)

(b) Calculate the work done by dragging the load up the ramp.

(2)

(c) The answer to (a) is the gain in gravitational potential energy of the load in each case. Explain why more work is needed to drag the load up the ramp than to lift it and suggest where the extra energy goes to.

....

....

.... (3)

(d) State **one** advantage of using the ramp instead of lifting the load.

.... (1)

4 A cycle and cyclist have a combined mass of 80 kg.

(a) Calculate the kinetic energy of the cycle and cyclist when travelling at a speed of 12 m/s.

....

.... (2)

(b) The cyclist applies a constant braking force and comes to rest after 8.0 s.

(i) Calculate the power of the brakes.

....

.... (2)

(ii) The braking distance is 48 m. Calculate the size of the braking force required.

....

....

.... (3)

(iii) Calculate the kinetic energy of the cycle and cyclist when travelling at a speed of 6 m/s.

....

.... (2)

(iv) Explain why, when the same braking force is applied, the braking distance from a speed of 6 m/s is 12 m.

.... (1)

17 Radioactivity

Radiation is all around us in the form of **background radiation**. Some of this comes from space, some from rocks and some from the radioactive carbon in us and every other living thing. Radioctive decay occurs when an unstable nucleus emits energy in the form of electromagnetic radiation or a particle when it changes to a more stable nucleus. The table summarises the three main types of radiation that can be emitted.

type of nuclear radiation	nature	charge	penetration	ionising ability
alpha	two neutrons and two protons, sometimes referred to as a helium nucleus	positive	stopped by a few cm of air or a thin piece of card	intensely ionising
beta	high-speed electron emitted when a neutron decays to a proton and an electron	negative	partially absorbed by aluminium foil; totally absorbed by 5 mm aluminium	less than alpha; ionisation occurs at collisions with atoms and molecules
gamma	high-frequency, short-wavelength electromagnetic radiation	none	never totally absorbed; intensity is reduced by thick lead or concrete	weakly ionising; the high penetration is due to few collisions where ionisation would occur

Many elements exist in different forms called **isotopes**, some of which are more stable than others. The different isotopes of an element have the same electron arrangement and the same number of protons but differ in the number of neutrons. The most common form of carbon is carbon-12 (the 12 refers to the total number of protons and neutrons) but the isotope carbon-14, an unstable form of carbon, also exists in nature. The table compares the isotopes.

isotope	electron arrangement	number of protons	number of neutrons
carbon-12	2, 4	6	6
carbon-14	2, 4	6	8

When carbon-14 decays it emits a beta particle as a neutron becomes a proton and the atom changes to a nitrogen atom.

$$^{14}_{6}C \rightarrow \,^{14}_{7}N + \,^{0}_{-1}e$$

Note that in the symbolic equation the top number to the left of the atomic symbol represents the **mass number**, or total number of protons and neutrons, and the bottom number is the **atomic number**, or number of protons.

Carbon-14 decays with a **half-life** of 5730 years. This means that, on average, half of the carbon-14 atoms in a sample of carbon change to nitrogen during this time. After one half-life of a material half of the unstable atoms are still present and the rate of decay has halved. These numbers halve again to a quarter of the original value after a second half-life and so on.

All living things contain a constant proportion of carbon-14; when they die they stop taking in new supplies of carbon-14 and so the proportion goes down as the carbon-14 decays. The time since the death of plant or animal material can be estimated by measuring the proportion of carbon-14 present and calculating the number of half-lives that have elapsed since death. This is a technique known as **radio-carbon dating**.

Substances with a long half-life, such as uranium-238 which has a half-life of 4500 million years, can be used to date rocks. Uranium-238 decays to lead, enabling the age of a rock to be estimated from the proportions of lead and uranium-238 present.

Radioactive isotopes are widely used in medicine for detecting and treating illness, for killing bacteria and for tracing the movement of fluids.

Nuclear power relies on the energy released when a large, unstable nucleus is split, or 'fissioned', into smaller ones. The splitting of the nucleus is triggered when a neutron is absorbed. As well as energy, other neutrons are released which can go on to cause more fissions.

If you need to revise this subject more thoroughly, see the relevant topics in the *Letts* GCSE Science Study Guide or CD-ROM.

1 (a) A Geiger-Müller tube is connected to a counter. It measures the background radiation each 60 s for ten successive time intervals. The table shows the results.

recording	1	2	3	4	5	6	7	8	9	10
number of counts in 60 s	62	59	69	67	61	68	68	70	72	64

(i) Name **two** sources of background radiation.

....

.... (2)

(ii) Explain why there is variation in the number of counts recorded in successive intervals.

.... (1)

(iii) Calculate a value for the average background radiation in counts/s.

.... (1)

(b) The same Geiger-Müller tube is used to measure the activity of a radioactive liquid containing protactinium-234, an isotope that has a half-life of around one minute. Readings of the activity are recorded at 10 s time intervals for a period of 2 minutes. The table shows the results.

time/s	0	10	20	30	40	50	60	70	80	90	100	110	120
count rate/ counts per s	32.2	30.0	27.7	25.2	22.6	20.9	19.2	17.3	15.9	14.8	13.4	12.1	11.0
corrected count rate/counts per s													

(i) Use your answer to (a) (iii) to complete the data in the table. (1)

(ii) Use the data to plot a graph of corrected count rate against time. (3)

(iii) Use your graph to obtain a value for the half-life of protactinium-234.

Explain how you arrive at your answer.

....

.... (2)

2 $^{12}_{6}$C and $^{14}_{6}$C are both isotopes of carbon.

(a) (i) Write down one similarity about the nucleus of each isotope.

.... (1)

(ii) Write down one difference in the nucleus of these isotopes.

.... (1)

(b) $^{14}_{6}$C is radioactive. It decays by emitting a beta particle.

(i) Describe a beta particle.

.... (2)

(ii) Which part of the atom emits the beta particle?

.... (1)

(c) $^{14}_{6}$C is present in all living materials and in all materials that have been alive. It decays with a half-life of 5 730 years.

(i) Explain the meaning of the term half-life.

....

.... (2)

(ii) The activity of a sample of wood from a freshly-cut tree is measured to be 80 counts/s.

Estimate the activity of the sample after two half-lives have elapsed.

.... (1)

(iii) The age of old wood can be estimated by measuring its radioactivity. Explain why this method cannot be used to work out the age of a piece of furniture made in the nineteenth-century .

....

.... (2)

*Try to complete this paper in one sitting of **one and a half hours**.*

1 The table gives some information about six elements.
These elements are lettered **A–F**.
These letters are *not* their chemical symbols.

element	melting point °C	boiling point °C	electron arrangement
A	−220	−188	2,7
B	−270	−269	2
C	3730	4830	2,4
D	98	890	2,8,1
E	850	1487	2,8,8,2
F	−101	−35	2,8,7

(a) Write down the letters of two elements in the same group of the Periodic Table.

.... (1)

(b) Write down the letters of two elements in the same period of the Periodic Table.

.... (1)

(c) Which element is liquid over the smallest range of temperature? .... (1)

(d) The diagrams show four arrangements of atoms.

Which diagram gives the arrangement of atoms in B at room temperature? .... (1)

(e) **C** conducts electricity.
Which other two elements conduct electricity? .... (2)

(f) (i) Draw diagrams to show the arrangement of outer electrons when
     D reacts with **A**   and   **C** reacts with **F**

(2)

(ii) What type of bonding is present in each of these compounds?

Compound of **D** and **A** ....

Compound of **C** and **F** .... (2)

2 This question is about the reaction of zinc with dilute hydrochloric acid. Hydrogen gas is also produced.

(a) Write a balanced symbol equation for this reaction.

(2)

(b) The table gives the conditions used for five experiments using zinc and dilute hydrochloric acid

experiment	sample of zinc/	volume of acid /cm³	volume of water /cm³	temperature °C	time/ minutes
1	1.0g of zinc lumps	50	0	20	3.0
2	1.0g of zinc powder	50	0	20	
3	1.0g of zinc lumps	50	50	20	
4	1.0g of zinc powder	50	0	40	
5	1.0g of zinc lumps	50	0	40	

(i) Which of the experiments will be finished in less than three minutes? .... (2)

(ii) Why is the volume of hydrogen collected the same in each experiment?

.... (1)

(iii)When experiment 1 was repeated with a few drops of copper(II) sulphate added, the reaction is finished in less than two minutes. Explain why.

....

....

.... (4)

(iv) Put a ring around a metal in the list which will react faster than zinc in similar experiments.

copper   iron   lead   magnesium (1)

3 Sam carried out some experiments to find the solubility of potassium nitrate in water at different temperatures.

Here are her results.

temperature °C	10	20	30	40	50	60	70	80	90
solubility g/100g water	21	32	45	61	83	106	135	167	203

(a) (i) Plot these results on a sheet of graph paper. (2)

(ii) Draw the best line through these points. (1)

(b) How does the solubility of potassium nitrate change with temperature?

....

.... (2)

(c) A saturated solution of potassium nitrate containing 50 g of water at 80° C is cooled to 20° C.
What mass of crystals will be formed? Show your working.

.... (2)

(d) The table gives the composition of four solutions of potassium nitrate.
For each solution finish the table by adding the word *saturated* or the word *unsaturated*.
One has been done for you.

solution	mass of potassium nitrate/g	mass of water/g	temperature/°C	saturated or unsaturated
W	50	100	40	unsaturated
X	50	400	20	
Y	50	50	50	
Z	50	200	30	

(3)

4   An experiment was carried out to investigate gaseous exchange between living organisms and their environment.
Four pieces of pondweed were used of equal mass. Six pond snails and hydrogencarbonate indicator were also used.
The table gives the colour of hydrogencarbonate indicator in solutions containing different concentrations of carbon dioxide.

Concentration of carbon dioxide	colour of hydrogencarbonate indicator
similar to concentration in normal air	red
very high	yellow
very low	purple

Four test tubes were set up, each containing a piece of pondweed and equal volumes of hydrogencarbonate indicator. Three snails were put in tube B and three in tube D.
The diagram shows the conditions in each tube.

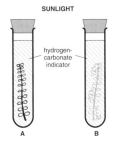
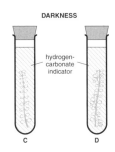

SUNLIGHT   DARKNESS

hydrogen-carbonate indicator

A   B   C   D

Finish the table by describing and explaining the concentration of carbon dioxide in each tube.

tube	colour after 4 hours	concentration of carbon dioxide	Explanation
A			
B			
C			
D			

(6)

5 To increase milk yields in India, native Zebu cows are mated with Friesian bulls from Great Britain. The cross-bred cows produce more milk for a longer period than Zebu cows.

(a) Suggest a cheaper way of doing this than transporting Friesian bulls from Great Britain to India.

.... (2)

(b) The diagram shows how a cross-bred embryo is produced.
Finish the diagram by adding the names of the types of nuclear division taking place.

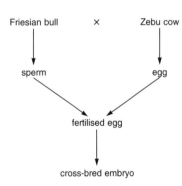

Type of nuclear division

....

Type of nuclear division

.... (2)

(c) The genotype of a hornless bull is **BB**.
The genotype of a horned cow is **bb**.

(i) What is the genotype of their cross-bred (F1) offspring?................................... (1)

(ii) A cross-bred (F1) cow and a cross-bred (F1) bull were mated.
What are the possible genotypes of their offspring (F2)?
Use a genetic diagram to explain your answer.

(3)

(d) Describe how a herd of hornless cattle could be developed.

....

.... (3)

6 Electric toasters and grills are heated when a current passes in them.
The size of the current depends on the voltage and the resistance.

(a) Write down the effect on the current of increasing

(i) the voltage .... (1)

(ii) the resistance. .... (1)

(b) A heating element has a resistance of 24 Ω.
Calculate the voltage across the element when a current of 5 A passes in it

(3)

(c) Most of the energy given off from the heating element in an electric toaster or grill is in
the form of electromagnetic radiation.
Name two types of electromagnetic radiation that are emitted by a red-hot grill.

1 ....

2 .... (2)

7 A cyclist travels a distance of 162.5 m in a time of 25 s.

(a) (i) Calculate the average speed of the cyclist.

(3)

(ii) Explain why this is an **average** speed.

....

.... (1)

During part of the cycle ride, the cyclist's speed increases from 3 m/s to 6 m/s in a 5 s time interval.

(b) Calculate the acceleration of the cyclist during this 5 s time interval.

.... (3)

(c) (i) Calculate the size of the unbalanced force needed to cause this acceleration. The combined mass of the cycle and cyclist is 85 kg.

(3)

(ii) Explain why the force pushing the cycle in the forwards direction needs to be greater than the correct answer to (c) (i).

.... (2)

8 (a) Complete the diagrams to show the path taken by light passing through a glass window and a triangular glass prism.

(2)

(b) When light enters the glass its speed is reduced.

(i) Write down the name of this effect. .... (1)

(ii) What is the effect on the wavelength of the light? .... (1)

(iii) What is the effect on the frequency of the light?... (1)

9 There are four processes that transfer energy from hot objects to cooler objects: conduction, convection, radiation and evaporation. Write down the main method of energy transfer for each example.

(i) A central heating radiator heats the air in a room.. (1)

(ii) Energy flows through the plasterboard ceiling of a warm bedroom into the

cold roof space. .... (1)

(iii) Energy from the Sun reaches the Earth. .... (1)

(iv) The skin temperature of a swimmer drops when she gets out of the swimming bath.

.... (1)

Many students taking GCSE Science are entered for Modular GCSE schemes offered by three of the Examination Groups. In all cases students take short tests during the course and the results are added together. These marks give 25% of the total mark, with 50% coming from the examinations at the end of the course and 25% from the assessment of practical skills (Sc1).

The modules used by the Examination Groups are different and so are the types of question used. All of the questions are multiple choice or objective questions that can be marked by machine.

This section will look at the schemes of the three Examination Groups and give examples of the types of questions used.

Hints when taking Modular GCSE Science Examinations

1 Remember module tests largely examine your knowledge and understanding. Make sure you learn the facts within the module thoroughly.

2 Either all of the content or part of the content (in the case of NEAB) is examined again in the examinations at the end of the course.

3 Read the questions carefully. Often mistakes occur when the student misreads the question.

4 If you cannot answer a question immediately, leave it out and come back to it.

5 There is no penalty if you get a question wrong. You must answer every question. If you can rule out two of the possible answers you have increased your answers of guessing correctly.

6 Do not go back at the end of the examination and change all your answers. Research shows students change more correct answers to incorrect ones than vice versa.

Remember that good results throughout the course will help you to achieve the grade you desire. However, the examination papers at the end of the course count twice as much as all the module tests.

NEAB MODULAR SCIENCE

Double Award Science

You will take six module tests during the course. Each module test will be offered at Higher and Foundation levels. Each module test takes 30 minutes. The titles of the modules are as follows:

1 Humans as organisms	**4** Earth Materials
2 Maintenance of Life	**5** Energy
3 Metals	**6** Electricity

Three types of questions are used in NEAB Modular tests. Your answers are recorded on a special answer sheet.

Single Award Science

You will take three module tests during the course. Each module test will be offered at Higher and Foundation levels. Each module test takes 30 minutes. The titles of the modules are as follows:

13 Life and Living Processes	**15** Materials from Oils and Ores
17 Energy and Electricity	

The same three types of questions are used as for Double Award.

Type 1

In this type there is one correct answer to match each option. Each option is used once.

Question 1

The table is about extraction of metals.

Match the words from the list with each of the numbers 1–4 in the table.

aluminium   copper   gold   iron

Metal	
1	purified by electrolysis
2	extracted from its ore in a blast furnace
3	found as the metal in the Earth
4	extracted from its ore by electrolysis

Record the correct answers by marking the correct boxes with a thick pencil stroke.

Question 1	1	2	3	4
aluminium	☐	☐	☐	☐
copper	☐	☐	☐	☐
gold	☐	☐	☐	☐
iron	☐	☐	☐	☐

Type 2

Here there are two correct answers to each question.

Question 2

This question is about the job of a fuse in a circuit.

Which two of the following are true about a fuse?

melts if the current becomes too great

is always placed in the neutral lead

controls the current passing in the circuit

protects the cable from overheating and catching fire

stops the appliance blowing up

Record the correct answers by marking the correct boxes with a thick pencil stroke.

Question 2	
melts if the current becomes too great	☐
is always placed in the neutral lead	☐
controls the current passing in the circuit	☐
protects the cable from overheating and catching fire	☐
stops the appliance blowing up	☐

Type 3
Here there are a series of four multiple choice questions about one situation.
Each question has four answers – one correct and three incorrect.

Question 3
The table shows information about four metals P, Q, R and S.
(These are not their chemical symbols).

Metal	Reaction with cold water	Reaction with dilute hydrochloric acid	Reaction with air on heating
P	No reaction	No reaction	Forms a black surface coating
Q	Very slow. Few bubbles of colourless gas	Steady reaction forming bubbles of colourless gas	Burns with bright flame leaving white solid
R	No reaction	Very slow reaction forming bubbles of colourless gas	Burns to form white solid
S	Steady reaction. Forms bubbles of colourless gas	Very rapid reaction forming bubbles of colourless gas	Burns to form white solid

3.1 Which one of the following shows the correct order of reactivity with the most reactive first?

A P R Q S   **B** S Q R P   **C** S Q P R   **D** Q S R P

3.2 Which metal will form the oxide with the highest pH value?

A P   **B** Q   **C** R   **D** S

3.3 Pieces of the four metals are put into separate solutions of the nitrate of P.
In how many test tubes will a reaction take place?

A none   **B** one   **C** two   **D** three

3.4 In several cases in the table, bubbles of colourless gas are observed.
What is the name of this gas?

A carbon dioxide   **B** hydrogen   **C** nitrogen   **D** oxygen

Record the correct answers by marking the correct boxes with a thick pencil stroke.

Question 3	A	B	C	D
3.1	☐	☐	☐	☐
3.2	☐	☐	☐	☐
3.3	☐	☐	☐	☐
3.4	☐	☐	☐	☐

SEG MODULAR SCIENCE

You are required to take nine modular tests during the course. Each test lasts 20 minutes. Each test will have eighteen questions and each question is worth 1 mark. There are two tiers or levels of papers – Foundation and Higher. Some questions will be on both tiers.

The titles of the nine module tests are:

1 Maintenance of life
2 Maintenance of species
3 Structure and changes
4 Forces and transfers
5 Energy sources

6 Vital exchanges
7 Bonding and materials
8 Using power
9 Universal changes

All questions will be of a similar type.
A sample question is:

Which gas is formed when methane burns in air?

A Carbon dioxide   **B** Hydrogen   **C** Nitrogen   **D** Oxygen

The four answers are arranged in alphabetical order. If the four answers are numbers they are arranged in numerical order.

The correct answer is **A** and this should be recorded on the answer sheet.

Here is a selection of questions similar to those on SEG Science papers.
Record the answers to these questions on the answer grid on page 102 using a thick pencil stroke.

QUESTIONS

Module 1

1 Which part of the blood transports oxygen round the body?

A Plasma   **B** Platelets   **C** Red blood cells   **D** White blood cells

2 Which part of a plant cell contains the genetic information?

A Cell membrane   **B** Cell wall   **C** Cytoplasm   **D** Nucleus

Module 2

3 A human skin cell contains 46 chromosomes.
How many chromosomes are there in a human egg cell?

A 23   **B** 42   **C** 46   **D** 92

4 When a gardener grows sweet peas using the seed he collected from plants that he grew the previous year, the new plants are:

A the same colour and size as the previous year   **B** the same colour but a different size
C quicker to grow   **D** different colours

Module 3

5 The elements in the modern Periodic Table are arranged in order of:

A atomic mass   **B** atomic number   **C** date of discovery   **D** number of neutrons

6 Bromine water is used to show the presence of:

    A a carbon–carbon double bond   **B** a chloride   **C** a hydrocarbon   **D** water

Module 4

7 Resistance is measured in:

    A amps   **B** ohms   **C** volts   **D** watts

8 An object moving at terminal velocity is:

    A accelerating downwards   **B** accelerating upwards
    C slowing down   **D** moving at a constant speed

Module 5

9 Which of the following are radioactive emissions?

    A alpha particles   **B** infra-red radiation   **C** microwaves   **D** ultra-violet radiation

10 Which object is the source of light in the Solar System?

    A The Earth   **B** Mars   **C** The Moon   **D** The Sun

Module 6

11 In the food chain: **grass** → **rabbit** → **fox**, the rabbit is a:

    A carnivore   **B** decomposer   **C** herbivore   **D** producer

12 Which of the following gases is used up in photosynthesis?

    A Carbon dioxide   **B** Chlorophyll   **C** Hydrogen   **D** Oxygen

Module 7

13 There are three isotopes of hydrogen: hydrogen-1, hydrogen-2 and hydrogen-3.
They contain different numbers of:

    A electrons   **B** protons   **C** protons and electrons   **D** protons and neutrons

14 What is the relative formula mass of calcium hydroxide, $Ca(OH)_2$?
(Relative atomic masses: $H = 1, O = 16, Ca = 40$.)

    A 57   58   **C** 73   **D** 74

Module 8

15 A relay is a device that:

    A changes an alternating current into a direct current
    B changes a direct current into an alternating current
    C uses a small current to switch a greater current
    D uses a large current to switch a smaller current

16 When the frequency of a note played by a keyboard is increased:

    A the note sounds quieter   **B** the note sounds louder
    C the note sounds lower pitched   **D** the note sounds higher pitched

Module 9

17 Which gas is not normally present in the air?

    A Argon   **B** Carbon dioxide   **C** Hydrogen   **D** Nitrogen

18 Carbon dioxide is formed when dilute acid is added to some rocks. Which rock would give carbon dioxide?

    A Basalt   **B** Chalk   **C** Granite   **D** Sandstone

Answer grid

1	A	B	C	D		10	A	B	C	D
2	A	B	C	D		11	A	B	C	D
3	A	B	C	D		12	A	B	C	D
4	A	B	C	D		13	A	B	C	D
5	A	B	C	D		14	A	B	C	D
6	A	B	C	D		15	A	B	C	D
7	A	B	C	D		16	A	B	C	D
8	A	B	C	D		17	A	B	C	D
9	A	B	C	D		18	A	B	C	D

EDEXCEL MODULAR SCIENCE

Double Award Science

The ten modules that make up the course are:

1 Body maintenance
2 Inheritance and survival
3 Understanding ecosystems
4 Chemicals and the Earth
5 Materials chemistry
6 Chemical patterns
7 Science in sport
8 Electricity and waves in the home
9 Applications of sound and electricity
10 Energy and gravitation

You will take a twenty-minute multiple choice test on each module. Each test consists of twenty multiple-choice questions. Each modular test can be taken at Foundation or Higher level, though you do not need to take all the tests at the same level. This means that if you start off taking the tests at Foundation level, you may move to Higher level tests if you improve during the course.

Here is a selection of questions similar to those on Edexcel modular test papers. Record your answers by striking through the correct letter on the answer sheet at the end.

Single Award Science

You will take five module tests during the course. The tests are identical to those for Science Double Award and are based on units 1, 2, 6, 8 and 10 from the double award scheme.

Module 1

1 The job of blood plasma is to:

    A fight infection   **B** carry oxygen   **C** carry soluble substances   **D** help blood to clot

2 A reflex action:

    A is controlled by hormones   **B** enables the brain to think before responding
    C is a voluntary response to a stimulus   **D** is an involuntary response to a stimulus

Module 2

3 In sexual reproduction characteristics are inherited from:

    A the mother only   **B** the father only
    C both the mother and the father   **D** neither the mother nor the father

4 Genes are located:

    A in the cell wall   **B** in the cytoplasm   **C** in the cell membrane   **D** in the cell nucleus

Module 3

5 A plant absorbs water through its:

    A root hairs   **B** stem hairs   **C** leaf hairs   **D** flower hairs

6 Plants need nitrates to make:

    A glucose   **B** glycogen   **C** protein   **D** starch

Module 4

7 Impure copper can be purified by:

    A electrolysis   **B** heating it in air
    C heating it in carbon monoxide   **D** heating it with carbon

8 A sedimentary rock was formed:

    A at the same time as the Earth   **B** by collisions from meteors
    C by layers of silt being compressed   **D** from volcanic action

Module 5

9 The dyes in an ink can be separated by:

    A chromatography   **B** dissolving   **C** evaporation   **D** filtration

10 Ionic compounds have:

  A low melting points and low boiling points   **B** high melting points and high boiling points
  C low melting points and high boiling points   **D** high melting points and low boiling points

Module 6

11 Fluorine, chlorine, bromine and iodine are all:

    A alkali metals   **B** halogens   **C** noble gases   **D** transition metals

12 Cracking describes:

    A the formation of large molecules from small molecules
    B the formation of small molecules from large molecules
    C the splitting up of an atomic nucleus   **D** the joining together of two atomic nuclei

Module 7

13 Anaerobic respiration takes place:

A when there is an excess of water in the blood   **B** when there is a deficit of water in the blood
C when there is an excess of oxygen in the blood   **D** when there is a deficit of oxygen in the blood

14 A sprinter has kinetic energy due to her:

    A food   **B** movement   **C** position   **D** temperature

Module 8

15 A lamp is designed to transfer energy from electricity into:

    A heat   **B** light   **C** sound   **D** movement

16 Which type of electromagnetic wave is used to operate the remote control of a television?

    A infra-red   **B** microwave   **C** radio wave   **D** ultra violet radiation

Module 9

17 The reflection of a sound wave from a flat surface is called:

    A a decibel   **B** an echo   **C** refraction   **D** sonar

18 A transformer can be used to:

    A switch a large current, using a small current   **B** switch a small current, using a large current
    C make a direct voltage bigger   **D** make an alternating voltage bigger

Module 10

19 Energy transfer by convection:

    A takes place in a vacuum only   **B** takes place in a solid only
    C takes place in a liquid only   **D** takes place in both liquids and gases

20 Our Solar System is part of which galaxy?

    A Mars   **B** Mercury   **C** Milky Way   **D** Sombrero

Answer grid

1	A	B	C	D		11	A	B	C	D
2	A	B	C	D		12	A	B	C	D
3	A	B	C	D		13	A	B	C	D
4	A	B	C	D		14	A	B	C	D
5	A	B	C	D		15	A	B	C	D
6	A	B	C	D		16	A	B	C	D
7	A	B	C	D		17	A	B	C	D
8	A	B	C	D		18	A	B	C	D
9	A	B	C	D		19	A	B	C	D
10	A	B	C	D		20	A	B	C	D

Answers to modular tests

NEAB Answers
1 aluminium 4, copper 1, gold 3, iron 2; **2** Ticks in first and fourth boxes; **3.1** B; **3.2** D; **3.3** D; **3.4** B
SEG Answers
1 C; **2** D; **3** A; **4** D; **5** B; **6** A; **7** B; **8** D; **9** A; **10** D; **11** C; **12** A; **13** D; **14** D; **15** C; **16** D; **17** C; **18** B
Edexcel Answers
1 C; **2** D; **3** C; **4** D; **5** A; **6** C; **7** A; **8** C; **9** A; **10** B; **11** B; **12** B; **13** D; **14** B; **15** B; **16** A; **17** B; **18** D; **19** D; **20** C

Answers

1 LIFE PROCESSES

Question	Answer	Mark
1 (a)	The sperm tail propels or moves the sperm.	1
	The large amount of cytoplasm contains a food supply for the egg.	1
	The long nerve fibre enables the cell to reach distant parts of the body.	1
	The chloroplasts are for photosynthesis.	1
	The large area is for absorption of water.	1
(b)	Either order, 1 mark each:	
	cytoplasm and cell membrane.	2
(c)	sperm 23	1
	ovum 23	1
	neurone 46	1
	red blood cell 0	1

Examiner's tip   The sex cells have half the full complement of chromosomes, one from each pair. Mature red blood cells do not have a nucleus and do not divide by mitosis or meiosis. They are made in bone marrow.

Question	Answer	Mark
2 (a) (i)	excretion	1
(ii)	reproduction	1
(iii)	respiration	1

Examiner's tip   Candidates often confuse respiration and breathing. Respiration takes place in body cells; it describes the chemical reaction between glucose and oxygen that releases energy. Breathing, or ventilation, is a mechanical process.

Question	Answer	Mark
(b) (i)	Your diagrams should show:	
	the chromosomes duplicate within the nucleus,	1
	the nucleus separates into two,	1
	the whole cell splits into two.	1
(ii)	In meiosis, one cell divides into four.	1
	The new cells have half the number of chromosomes of the original cell.	1

Question	Answer	Mark
3 (a)	The completed graph is shown on the next page.	
	Marks are awarded for:	
	suitable scale and correct label, one mark each axis.	2
	best-fit curves drawn, 1 mark each curve.	3

Examiner's tip   No marks are awarded here if you joined the crosses with a series of straight lines. When drawing curves on graphs, draw your curve so that it represents the overall pattern. Candidates often weave the curve around to try to make it go through as many points as possible or draw the curve so that it goes through the first and last points. Except for cases where a reading is zero, as in this case, these are no more reliable than any other points on the graph.

Question	Answer	Mark
	all lines labelled	1

uptake of sulphate/counts per minute

aerobic

anaerobic

poison

time/minutes

(b)	The uptake of sulphate depends on the oxygen availability,	1
	and whether there is any metabolic poison present.	1
	This suggests that respiration is involved.	1
	Anaerobic respiration releases less energy than aerobic respiration so the uptake is slower.	1
	Active transport depends on the energy released in respiration.	1

Examiner's tip This is an example of a question where candidates need to use the evidence to assemble a logical argument and set this out in an extended piece of writing. This type of question will be common on Higher tier papers from 1998.

(c)	(i)	Diffusion is the net movement of the sulphate ions from an area of high concentration to one of low concentration.	1
	(ii)	The results for aerobic respiration would be similar to those for anaerobic respiration, the results in the presence of metabolic poison would be similar to those without poison, the uptake of sulphate would be less.	
		1 mark each for any two of these three points.	2

Examiner's tip If you answered that 'all the results would be similar' you have both of the first two points and so you gain both marks.

2 HUMANS

Question	Answer	Mark
1 (a)	The rate of metabolism increases.	1
	This releases energy.	1

Question			Answer	Mark
	(b)		Heat is produced during exercise.	1
			This has to be lost to keep the body temperature constant.	1
	(c)		Glucose from the blood is changed into glycogen.	1
			This is stored in the liver and muscles.	1
	(d)	(i)	The glucose level rises several times a day.	1
			The hormone level needs to increase at these times to remove the glucose.	1

Examiner's tip Answering this part of the question requires you to interpret the graph correctly.

		(ii)	Glucose is used in exercise.	1
			So less hormone is needed as there is less glucose to be removed from the blood.	1

2	(a)		It helps to protect against disease	1
			by killing microorganisms taken in with food.	1

Examiner's tip The question asks the candidates to explain, so it is not enough to state the purpose of the acid. To get full marks candidates also need to explain how it does the job.

	(b)	(i)	Mucus-producing cells cause a film of mucus.	1
			This traps microorganisms.	1
			The cilia move the mucus into the larynx.	1
			The mucus is swallowed.	1
		(ii)	The mucus traps dust and microorganisms.	1
			It is swallowed or ejected out of the nose.	1
	(c)	(i)	The cilia are unable to move the mucus along.	1
		(ii)	Microorganisms remain in the trachea where they can cause disease.	1

3	(a)		The oxidation of glucose/food	1
			releases energy, some of which is heat.	1
	(b)		Evaporation of sweat causes cooling.	1
			The evaporation rate is greater in a drier climate.	1

Examiner's tip Candidates are often confused about how sweating helps the body to get rid of excess energy. Sweat itself does not have a cooling effect, but it removes energy when it evaporates.

	(c)		It causes reduced blood flow near surface of skin.	1
			There is less energy lost.	1

Examiner's tip A common error when answering this question is to state that the blood vessels move further away from the skin. This is not the case; they become narrower as less blood flows near the surface.

Question	Answer	Mark
(d)	One mark for any four of the following five points:	
	The change in temperature is detected by sensors or the brain.	
	The processor is the hypothalamus.	
	Nerve impulses are sent to the muscles.	
	Contraction of the muscles raises the temperature.	
	The effect of feedback stops shivering.	4

Examiner's tip When a person shivers, the muscles alternately contract and relax. The work done when the muscles contract produces heat.

3 GREEN PLANTS AS ORGANISMS

Question	Answer	Mark
1 (a)	Any one of the following:	
	Leaves are broad.	
	Leaves are flat.	
	Leaves have a large surface area.	1

Examiner's tip These are all ways leaves have adapted. You will not be given marks for saying, for example, 'the cuticle is transparent', which is a piece of information given in (b) and not an adaptation.

(b)	(i)	This allows light through to the palisade layer.	1
	(ii)	This part of the leaf receives most light.	1
	(iii)	The air spaces allow oxygen and carbon dioxide to diffuse to and from the cells.	1

Examiner's tip The air spaces are also close to the stomata where gases enter and leave the leaf. This would be an acceptable alternative answer.

(c)		Chlorophyll	1
(d)	(i)	More light increases the rate of photosynthesis.	1
	(ii)	Lowering the temperature decreases the rate of photosynthesis.	1

Examiner's tip Here the question is about the rate of photosynthesis. Your answer should be in terms of increasing and decreasing the rate of photosynthesis. Weaker candidates answer in terms of the growth of the plant, e.g. 'the plant grows better'. This vagueness is not acceptable and would receive no credit.

(e)	carbon dioxide + water → carbohydrates + oxygen	1

2 (a)		The peas get more light;	1
		more photosynthesis takes place;	1
		this produces sweeter peas,	1
		and a higher yield.	1

Question	Answer	Mark

(b) (i) Any time in the range 12:00 to 18:00. 1

(ii) **X** 1

The carbon dioxide level increases earlier. 1

(c) One mark each for any two of the following points:

warmth, water, removing weeds, nutrients or fertiliser, suitable pH. 2

(d)

Order of stages	Letter
1	E
2	A
3	D
4	B

One mark for each correct letter. 3

4 VARIATION, INHERITANCE AND EVOLUTION

Question	Answer	Mark

1 (a) The farmers could have chosen the cows with a high milk yield, 1
and only bred from these cows. 1
This process would be repeated through several generations. 1

(b) Fewer cows are needed to produce the milk. 1
This uses less land/less food. 1

2 (a) A gene mutation occurred. 1
This could have been caused by a miscopy or radiation damage. 1

(b) The dark-coloured moths are camouflaged. 1
More have survived and reproduced. 1

Question	Answer		Mark
3 (a)	Father	= **XY**	1
	Eggs	= **X X** Sperms = **X Y**	1
	Daughter = **XX** Son = **XY**		1

Examiner's tip This diagram shows how the sex of a child is determined by the chromosomes it inherits from its father.

		Mark
(b)	**G** 1 in 2 or 50% **H** zero	1
	The gene for the disease must be dominant.	1
	Because two of the offspring of A and B show the symptoms, but only one parent has the disease.	1
	Children inherit one chromosome from each pair in each parent.	1
	So there is a 50:50 chance that the offspring of C and D will inherit the gene from their father.	1
	Neither E nor F has the disease, so they cannot have the gene, therefore H cannot inherit it.	1

Examiner's tip In this type of question there are more marks for explaining how you arrive at your answer than for the answer itself. Before writing your final answer, it is a good idea to jot down the main points you want to make and then put them in a logical order.

5 LIVING THINGS IN THE ENVIRONMENT

Question	Answer	Mark
1 (a) (i)	25	1
(ii)	Grasshoppers are cold blooded OR move less.	1

Examiner's tip Award the mark if you have answered that field mice are warm blooded or move more.

		Mark
(b) (i)	59200	1
(ii)	One mark each for any two of the following points:	
	Some is used in respiration OR movement.	
	Some is wasted in excretion.	
	Some went to decomposers.	
	Some was not digestible.	2

Examiner's tip Questions which test whether you understand how energy is lost at each trophic level are common in GCSE science papers.

		Mark
2 (a) (i)	**A**	1
	This pathway has the smallest number of trophic levels.	1

Question	Answer	Mark

Examiner's tip In a food chain or web approximately 10% of the energy is passed on from one trophic level to the next. The smaller the number of trophic levels, the less energy is lost to the surroundings.

(ii) **A** — 1

Starving populations tend to eat producers. — 1

Examiner's tip Eating producers gives a starving population the greatest amount of the available energy.

(iii) Either **B**

because warm blooded animals give off more heat to the environment.

Or **C** — 1

because there are more trophic levels. (Marks awarded for either answer.) — 1

Examiner's tip This is an example of a question where there is no absolutely correct answer: you need to give a reason that is correct for your choice of pathway.

(b) (i) There is only one rosebush but there are lots of greenfly and several ladybirds. — 1

The total mass of the rosebush is greater than that of the greenfly which is greater than that of the ladybirds. — 1

(ii) Any two points from the following:

The number of greenfly declines as they are eaten by the ladybirds.

This leads to a fall in the number of ladybirds as there is less food.

The number of greenfly declines in late summer as the temperature drops. — 2

(iii) Insect sprays are pollutants. — 1

Organisms can become resistant to sprays. — 1

6 STRUCTURE AND BONDING

Question	Answer	Mark

1 (a) Gas — 1

Examiner's tip Remember: there are three states of matter – solid, liquid and gas. Here, in a gas, the particles are widely spaced and moving rapidly.

(b) From left to right:

A compound–hydrogen bromide. — 1

A mixture of hydrogen and bromine gases. — 1

A mixture of hydrogen bromide, hydrogen and bromine. — 1

Examiner's tip This question is testing your understanding of elements, mixtures and compounds. In the molecules of the compound, atoms of hydrogen and bromine are combined. The third diagram is interesting. It represents either the situation during the reaction, when the hydrogen and bromine molecules are being used up and hydrogen bromide molecules are forming, or the system in equilibrium when the rates of the forward and reverse reactions are equal. Candidates often are not clear about the distinction between elements, mixtures and compounds.

Question	Answer	Mark

(c) (i)

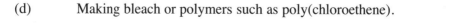

H Br

		2
	Covalent bonding.	1
(ii)	Covalent bond broken.	1
	Forms hydrogen ions and bromide ions.	1
	H^+ and $Br-$	1

2 (a)

Isotope	Mass Number	Abundance	Number of protons in one atom	Number of electrons in one atom	Number of neutrons in one atom
chlorine-35	35	75%	17	17	18
chlorine-37	37	25%	17	17	20

4

Examiner's tip It is important to use the Periodic Table to find the atomic number of chlorine – the number of protons and the number of electrons in a chlorine atom. All chlorine atoms contain 17p and 17e. You can now work out the number of neutrons.
In marking this there is a half mark for each correct answer but the examiner has to avoid half marks. The examiner will round up your mark so three correct answers will score 2 marks.

(b) (i) Every four chlorine atoms will have three chlorine-35 and one chlorine-37. **1**

Relative atomic mass $= \dfrac{(35 \times 3) + 37}{4}$ **1**

$= 35.5$

Examiner's tip There is no mark for the answer as this is given in the question.

(ii) 71 **1**

Examiner's tip A chlorine molecule is made up of two chlorine atoms.

(c)

$$\begin{matrix} \times\times & \times\times \\ \times\; Cl\; \times\; Cl\; \times \\ \times\;\;\;\;\times \\ \times\times & \times\times \end{matrix} \quad \textbf{or} \quad \begin{matrix} \times\times & \bullet\bullet \\ \times\; Cl\; \times\; Cl\; \bullet \\ \times\;\;\;\;\bullet \\ \times\times & \bullet\bullet \end{matrix}$$

2

Examiner's tip The common mistake here is to draw inner electrons, despite the instruction in the question. Chlorine is in Group 7 and therefore has seven outer electrons. The bonding in a chlorine molecule is covalent involving sharing or a pair of electrons.
One mark is for the shared pair of electrons. The second mark is for the other six non-bonding electrons in each chlorine atom.

(d) Making bleach or polymers such as poly(chloroethene). **1**

Question	Answer					Mark

3 (a)

Substance	Structure	Melting point	Electrical conductivity	
			Solid	Molten
diamond	giant covalent	high	poor	*poor*
magnesium chloride	ionic	high	*poor*	good
bromine	*covalent molecular*	low	poor	poor

3

(b)

$$\times^{\times}_{}{}^{\times}_{O}{}^{\times}_{}\times$$

× •
• ×
H   H

2

Examiner's tip This is another question on structure and bonding. Questions on this topic are often not well answered, so answer such questions with care.

7 OIL AND CARBON CHEMISTRY

Question	Answer	Mark
1 (a)	Natural gas	1
(b)	Exothermic reaction	1
(c)	Oxidation	1

Examiner's tip This is an oxidation reaction because hydrogen is lost when CH_3OH is converted into HCHO.

(d)	Large surface area for reaction to take place.	1
(e)	$CO(g) + 2H_2(g) \rightarrow CH_3OH(g)$	2

Examiner's tip 1 mark is awarded for getting the correct formulae for carbon monoxide, hydrogen and methanol in the correct place and the second mark is for balancing the equation. The state symbols are not necessary but if you use them you will not be penalised for a mistake. Note that methanol, which is a liquid at room temperature, is a gas at $300°\,C$.

(f)	Either as a material for making polymers or for synthetic petrol.	1

Examiner's tip In New Zealand, where there are supplies of natural gas but not petroleum, these processes are used to make synthetic petroleum.

2 (a)		Fractional distillation	1
(b)	(i)	Cracking	1
	(ii)	Polymerisation	1

Question	Answer	Mark
(c)	H—C—C—C—H (propane structure with H atoms)	1
(d)	All of the carbon–carbon bonds are single bonds.	1
(e)	Single bond between carbon atoms.	1
	Indication that many ethene bonds are joined together:	
	(polymer structure)	1

Examiner's tip Candidates frequently fail to score both marks in (e). Two marks for this part indicate that two points need to be made.

8 MATERIALS FROM ROCKS

Question	Answer	Mark
1 (a)	You have to choose suitable scales before you plot the points. You should try to fill the graph paper.	
	Suitable scales – on the y axis 200 km or 250 km to 2 cm, on the x axis 10 millions of years to 2 cm.	1
	Axes labelled with name and unit	1
	Correct plotting	1
	Straight line	1

(graph: Distance from ridge/km vs Age of sediments/millions of years, straight line through plotted points)

Examiner's tip Do not join the points on a graph with a straight line. Remember there will be some possibility of error with these results. Also, continue your line back to zero. When the age is zero, the distance moved will be zero.

| (b) | (i) | To find the rate of spreading find the gradient (steepness) by dividing distance by time e.g. $1600/80 = 20$ km/millions of years. | 1 |

Examiner's tip This graph you have drawn is a distance-time graph. When working out a gradient draw a large triangle.

Question		Answer	Mark
	(ii)	From your graph you should have a reading of approximately 50 million years.	1
(c)		Convection currents in the magma.	1
		Brings rocks to the surface.	1
		Lava or magma escapes through cracks, or pressure forces lava or magma up.	1
		Constructive plate boundary.	1
(d)		Less carbon dioxide when there is no volcanic activity so less photosynthesis takes place.	1
		Less oxygen or less food or global warming.	1

2 (a)		Reduction	1
(b)		$Fe_2O_3(s) + 3CO(g) \rightarrow 2Fe(l) + 3CO_2(g)$	2
		1 mark for correct formulae and 1 mark for balancing.	
(c)		Burning of coke.	1
		Hot air entering the furnace.	1

Examiner's tip The negative value for ΔH given for the combustion of carbon shows that the reaction is exothermic. The high temperature in the furnace is also maintained because the refractory bricks lining the furnace are poor conductors of heat. You would have scored a mark if you stated that.

(d)		Nitrogen and argon. (Both required)	1

Examiner's tip Other gases could be accepted. The waste gases could include carbon dioxide, unreacted oxygen, any other noble gas.

(e)		Adding impurities lowers the melting point.	1
(f)	(i)	120g	1
	(ii)	Mass of 1 mole of $SiO_2 = 28 + 16 + 16 = 60$g	1
		Number of moles of $SiO_2 = 120/60 = 2$	1
	(iii)	From the equations, 2 moles of SiO_2 require 2 moles of $CaCO_3$	1
		$= 200\,g$	1
		(N.B. Mass of 1 mole of $CaCO_3 = 100\,g$)	

Examiner's tip This question involves some quantitative chemistry (Chapter 9)

9 QUANTITATIVE CHEMISTRY

Question	Answer	Mark
1 (a)	$0.407 - 0.327 = 0.080\,g$	1
(b)	Number of moles of X $= {}^{0.327}/_{65.4} = 0.005$	1
	Number of moles of O $= {}^{0.80}/_{16} = 0.005$	1
	Simplest formula $= XO$	1

<table>
<tr><td>Examiner's tip</td><td>This type of calculation is common on Higher tier papers. If the answers gave, for example, 0.0025 moles of X and 0.005 moles of O, the simplest formula would be XO_2. This is because there are twice as many oxygen atoms as X atoms.</td></tr>
</table>

2 (a)	Plotting (see graph below).	2
	One mark is deducted if there is one wrong plot.	
	Line of best fit drawn.	1

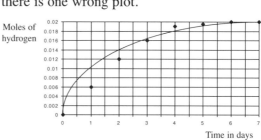

(b)	0.020 moles	1
(c)	From the equation 0.02 moles of hydrogen is produced by 0.02 moles of W.	1
(d)	0.02 moles of W has a mass of 0.48 g.	
	1 mole of W has a mass of 0.48/0.02 g.	1
	$= 24\,g$	1

<table>
<tr><td>Examiner's tip</td><td>It is a good idea now to check your Periodic Table. Magnesium has a relative atomic mass of 24. This means it has a mass of 1 mole of 24 g. It forms an oxide MgO and reacts only very slowly with water. All of this should give you more confidence about your answer.</td></tr>
</table>

3 (a)	(i)	A – air; B – natural gas or naphtha.	2
	(ii)	Iron is a catalyst.	1
(b)	(i)	$3H_2$; $2NH_3$. Both required.	1
	(ii)	Increasing pressure at constant temperature increases the percentage of ammonia.	1
		Increasing temperature at constant pressure decreases the percentage of ammonia.	1
		Best percentage would be at high pressure and low temperature.	1
		At low temperatures the reaction would be too slow.	1
		High pressures are expensive to produce.	1
		The conditions given are a compromise giving a good yield in a reasonable time and without excessive costs.	1

<table>
<tr><td>Examiner's tip</td><td>This answer is an example of a piece of extended writing. Notice there are six points and the answer has made six different points in a logical order.</td></tr>
</table>

Letts

Q&A

Question	Answer	Mark
(c)	Nitric acid.	1
(d) (i)	Farmers add ammonium nitrate as a fertiliser.	1
	It provides nitrogen which is an essential element for plant growth.	1
(ii)	Ammonium nitrate is washed into rivers.	1
	Ammonium nitrate removes oxygen dissolved in the water.	1

Examiner's tip You can improve the quality of your answer here by stating that ammonium nitrate is very soluble in water and by outlining steps in the river involving bacteria to remove dissolved oxygen.

10 THE PERIODIC TABLE

Question	Answer	Mark
1 (a) (i)	The atoms are most closely packed.	1

Examiner's tip It is important to make the link between density and close packing of atoms. In a gas the atoms are widely spaced so the density is low. In a metal, such as lead, the atoms are closely packed, giving a high density.

(ii)	Three	1
(b) (i)	Noble gases.	1
(ii)	Chart completed correctly	2
	(Award only one mark for a slight mistake).	

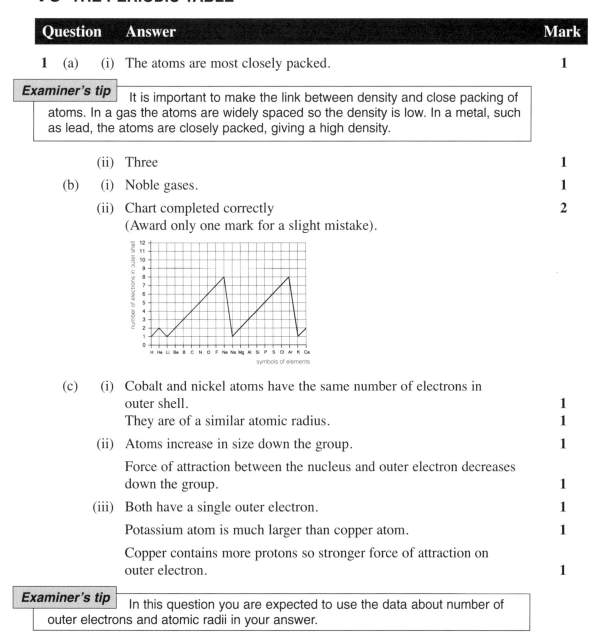

(c) (i)	Cobalt and nickel atoms have the same number of electrons in outer shell.	1
	They are of a similar atomic radius.	1
(ii)	Atoms increase in size down the group.	1
	Force of attraction between the nucleus and outer electron decreases down the group.	1
(iii)	Both have a single outer electron.	1
	Potassium atom is much larger than copper atom.	1
	Copper contains more protons so stronger force of attraction on outer electron.	1

Examiner's tip In this question you are expected to use the data about number of outer electrons and atomic radii in your answer.

11 RATES OF REACTION

Question	Answer	Mark

1 (a) (i) Ca   C   O   **3**

(ii) Carbon dioxide (not CO_2).   **1**

(b) (i)

Two marks for correct plotting.
One mark for drawing a curve.   **3**

(ii) Less carbon dioxide is produced with **X**.   **1**

(iii) As the reaction proceeds the concentration of the hydrochloric acid
is reduced.   **1**
Calcium carbonate reacts more slowly as the acid concentration decreases. **1**

---

2 (a) faster   zinc has a much larger surface area   **1**
faster   higher temperature. More particles have a
higher energy – more collisions exceed
activation energy   **1**
faster   more zinc – slightly larger surface area   **1**

(b) Reaction faster.   **1**
Magnesium is more reactive than zinc (or higher in the reactivity series).   **1**

(c) 0.5 g   **1**
A catalyst is not used up – mass unchanged.   **1**

(d) (i) Zinc sulphate.   **1**

(ii) Zinc nitrate.   **1**

12 ELECTRICITY AND MAGNETISM

Question	Answer	Mark
1 (a)	The petrol gains electrons	1
	from the metal pipe.	1
(b)	Positive.	1

> **Examiner's tip** All electrostatic charging is due to the transfer of electrons between objects. The outermost electrons in atoms and molecules are easily removed by the friction forces when objects rub together. A common error by GCSE candidates is to state that objects become positively charged by gaining protons.

(c)	The metal pipe becomes charged to a high voltage.	1
	This ionises the air between the pipe and the person's hand.	1
	The spark caused by charge passing through the air ignites the petrol.	1
(d)	The charge becomes spread out,	1
	so a high voltage does not occur.	1

> **Examiner's tip** High voltages can be caused by small amounts of charge if the charge is concentrated over a small area. Spreading the charge over a larger area reduces the voltage.

2 (a)	(i)	The lamp.	1
		The lamp has the smallest current.	1

> **Examiner's tip** If you calculated the resistance of the lamp, you also needed to calculate the resistance of the kettle and the toaster to make a comparison.

	(ii)	The kettle needs an earth wire.	1
		The cable is too thin to carry the high current to the kettle element.	1
(b)	(i)	Knowledge of formula $P = V \times I$	1
		$= 8.5\,A \times 240\,V = 2040$	1
		W	1

> **Examiner's tip** The last mark is for knowing the unit of power, so this mark can be awarded even if the answer is wrong.

	(ii)	4.25 A	1
	(iii)	The kettle takes longer to boil.	1
		It takes four times as long.	1

> **Examiner's tip** The kettle takes four times as long to boil because both the current and the voltage have been halved, so the power is only one quarter of the power when it is operated from a 240 V supply.

3 (a)	energy transfer = power x time = 2.5 kW x 1.5 h x 90	1
	= 337.5 kWh	1

Question	Answer	Mark
	cost = 337.5 kWh x 7 p/kWh = 2362.5 p or £23.625	**1**

Examiner's tip The energy formula is not one that you are required to know. It will be given in the question or on a separate formula sheet. The same formula is used for calculating energy transfer in joules when the power is in watts and the time in seconds.

(b)	The heater is fitted with a thermostat	**1**
	so it is not heating the water for 12 hours.	**1**

Examiner's tip The thermostat is an additional switch in series with the main switch; it turns the heater off when the pre-set temperature has been reached and on again when the water cools to a few degrees below this temperature.

(c)	(i)	The live conductor carries energy to the heater.	**1**
		The neutral completes the circuit.	**1**
	(ii)	The earth wire is connected to the metal casing,	**1**
		if this becomes live there is a low-resistance path to earth.	**1**
		The resulting high current melts the fuse and breaks the circuit.	**1**

Examiner's tip Always try to use the correct technical and scientific terms; in this case it is correct to state that the fuse 'melts' rather than 'blows'.

4	(a)	Any two from:	
		change the voltage,	
		change the length or diameter of the carbon rod,	
		adjust the setting of the variable resistor. 1 mark each.	**2**

Examiner's tip A common error on this type of question is to answer 'use a bigger battery or power supply'. This does not gain a mark as it is the voltage, rather than the physical size, that determines the current in the circuit.

(b) (i) Your completed graph should look like this:

voltage V (vertical axis, 0 to 5); current A (horizontal axis, 0 to 5)

Award marks for:

suitable scales and correct labels on the axes,	**1**
correct plotting of all the points,	**1**
drawing a smooth curve.	**1**

Question	Answer	Mark

(ii) 2.4 V **1**

(iii) knowledge of formula   resistance = voltage ÷ current **1**

$$= 2.4\,V \div 1.5\,A$$ **1**

$$= 1.6\,\Omega$$ **1**

5 (a) (i) power = current × voltage or P = I × V **1**

(ii) power = 6 V × 0.3 A **1**

$$= 1.8\,W$$ **1**

(b) A voltage is produced in the secondary coil when the magnetic field from the primary coil changes. **1**

With a steady direct current in the primary, the magnetic field does not change. **1**

(c) The output voltage is 1/40 of the input. **1**

So the secondary coil has 1/40 the number of turns of the primary. **1**

Which is 8000 ÷ 40 = 200 **1**

6 (a) The needle moves indicating a current. **1**

(b) The needle stays at zero. **1**

(c) The needle moves. **1**

The movement is in the opposite direction from that in (a). **1**

13 FORCES AND MOTION

Question		Answer	Mark
1	(i)	A speeding up or accelerating. B travelling at a constant speed. C speeding up or accelerating. D slowing down to a halt.	1 1 1 1
	(ii)	Knowledge of formula distance travelled $= $ speed $\times$ time $\qquad = 8\,\text{m/s} \times 17\,\text{s}$ $\qquad = 136\,\text{m}$	1 1 1
	(iii)	Knowledge of formula acceleration $=$ increase in velocity $\div$ time taken $\qquad = 8\,\text{m/s} \div 9\,\text{s}$ $\qquad = 0.89\,\text{m/s}^2$	1 1 1
	(iv)	Knowledge of formula force $=$ mass $\times$ acceleration $\qquad = 95\,\text{kg} \times 0.89\ \text{m/s}^2$ $\qquad = 84.4\ \text{N}$	1 1 1
	(v)	As the cyclist goes faster the resistive forces increase. This reduces the size of the unbalanced force and so the acceleration decreases.	1 1

Examiner's tip If the resistive forces have a value of 20 N this reduces the effective forwards force to 64.4 N.

	(vi)	Knowledge of formula: Acceleration $=$ increase in velocity $\div$ time taken $\qquad = -12 \div 15 = -0.8\,\text{m/s}^2$	 1 1

Examiner's tip The force is calculated using the formula force = mass × acceleration; first the acceleration has to be calculated, using the data from the graph. The minus sign shows that it is a deceleration and can be ignored.

		Force $=$ mass $\times$ acceleration $\qquad = 95 \times 0.8$ $\qquad = 76\,\text{N}$	1 1
	(vii)	Knowledge of formula: distance $=$ average speed $\times$ time $\qquad = 6\ \text{m/s} \times 15\,\text{s}$ $\qquad = 90\ \text{m}$	1 1 1
	(viii)	Time taken to stop $= 7.5\,\text{s}$ Distance travelled $= 3\,\text{m/s} \times 7.5\,\text{s}$ $\qquad = 22.5\,\text{m}$	1 1 1

Examiner's tip For the same force, the time taken to stop from a speed of 6 m/s would be half that taken to stop from a speed of 12 m/s.

	(ix)	Braking from 12 m/s takes twice as long as from 6 m/s and the average speed while braking is twice as much. These factors combine to make the braking distance four times as great.	1 1 1
2	(a)	knowledge of formula pressure $=$ force $\div$ area	1

Question	Answer	Mark
	$= 200\,\text{N} \div 20\,\text{cm}^2 = 10\,\text{N/cm}^2$	1
(b)	$10\,\text{N/cm}^2$	1

> **Examiner's tip** Fluids transmit pressure equally in all directions, so when the oil is put under pressure, the pressure is the same at all points in the oil.

(c)	force = pressure × area	1
	$= 10\,\text{N/cm}^2 \times 400\,\text{cm}^2 = 4000\,\text{N}$	1

> **Examiner's tip** The first mark here is for a correct rearrangement of the pressure formula.

(d) (i)	volume of cylinder = cross-sectional area × height	1
	$= 20\,\text{cm}^2 \times 2\,\text{cm} = 40\,\text{cm}^3$	1
(ii)	distance = volume ÷ area	1
	$= 40\,\text{cm}^3 \div 400\,\text{cm}^2 = 0.1\,\text{cm}$	1

> **Examiner's tip** This is testing whether you appreciate that the same volume of oil pushed out of the centre cylinder on the diagram is pushed into the right hand cylinder.

(iii)	That the oil does not compress.	1

> **Examiner's tip** When solids and liquids are put under pressure, there is very little change in volume, because the particles are very close-packed. Bubbles of air must not be allowed to enter a hydraulic system because they are easily compressed when pressure is applied, and this compression reduces the volume of oil that moves.

3 (a)	The sky diver's weight or the Earth's pull.	1
	Acts downwards.	1
	Air resistance.	1
	Acts upwards.	1

> **Examiner's tip** Avoid using the term 'gravity' when describing forces. The force between the sky diver and the Earth is a gravitational force because it is due to their masses, but the Earth is the actual object that pulls on the sky diver.

(b)	The last part, where the curve is parallel to the time axis.	1
(c)	The acceleration is decreasing	1
	and is zero towards the end of the graph.	1

> **Examiner's tip** The gradient of a speed-time graph represents the acceleration. The gradient of the graph decreases to zero, representing an acceleration that also decreases to zero; i.e. the sky diver travels at a constant speed.

Question	Answer	Mark
(d)	The downward force (weight) stays constant but the upward force increases as the sky diver travels faster.	1
	As the upward force increases, the size of the unbalanced force, and therefore the acceleration, decreases.	1
	When the upward and downward forces are equal in size the unbalanced force on the skydiver is zero, so there is no acceleration.	1
4 (a)	325 cm³	1
(b)	$P_1V_1 = P_2V_2$ so $P_2 = \dfrac{P_1V_1}{V_2}$ $= \dfrac{5.0 \times 10^5 \text{ Pa} \times 175 \text{ cm}^3}{325 \text{ cm}^3}$ $= 2.7 \times 10^5 \text{ Pa}$	3

Examiner's tip Candidates frequently make errors on this type of question because they cannot manipulate the equation. It is worthwhile practising rearranging the equations that you are required to know and be able to use at GCSE.

14 WAVES

Question	Answer	Mark
1 (a) (i)	A	1
(ii)	B	1
(b) (i)	The pressure decreases from P to Q.	1
	It is greatest at P and smallest at Q.	1
(ii)	The air particles vibrate or oscillate.	1
	Parallel to the direction of wave travel.	1

Examiner's tip A common error is to omit the last point. The question is testing whether you know that sound is a longitudinal wave.

(iii)	The marked distance should include a compression and a rarefaction and be twice the distance between P and Q.	1
2 (a) (i)	Light from the Sun is reflected by the tree.	1
(ii)	Your diagram should show light from the tree being reflected at the water surface so that the angle of incidence is equal to the angle of reflection.	1
(iii)	The image should be: Directly below the tree, each point being the same distance below the level of the water surface as the actual tree is above it.	1
	Upside down.	1
	The same size as the tree.	1

Question	Answer	Mark
(iv)	The image is a virtual one.	1
	Light appears to have come from the image, but it has not really come from there.	1
(b)	This is what the completed diagrams should look like:	

	The marks are for:	
	Left-hand diagram: reduced wavelength	1
	no change in direction.	1
	Right-hand diagram: reduced wavelength	1
	correct change in direction.	1

3 (a)	Any two from ultra-violet, X-rays and gamma rays.	1 mark each	**2**
(b)	**ultra-violet**		
(i)	Emitted by mercury vapour lamps or comes from the Sun.		**1**
(ii)	Used on sunbeds or to reveal security marking or in fluorescent lights.		**1**
(iii)	Can cause skin cancer.		**1**
(iv)	Keep the skin covered.		**1**
	X-rays		
(i)	Comes from X-ray tubes.		**1**
(ii)	Used to examine bones or other body organs or to treat cancer.		**1**
(iii)	Causes damage to healthy cells.		**1**
(iv)	Avoid the X-ray beam or wear lead-lined protective clothing.		**1**
	gamma rays		
(i)	Come from unstable nuclei.		**1**
(ii)	Used for sterilising medical instruments or examining welds or treating cancer.		**1**
(iii)	Causes damage to healthy cells.		**1**
(iv)	Do not get close to the source, or wear lead-lined protective clothing, or monitor exposure to the radiation to make sure that 'safe' levels are not exceeded.		**1**

Examiner's tip Extended writing has been a key feature of science examinations since 1998. You will be expected to be able to write a description or put forward a logical argument where several points have to be made. Candidates often fail to gain marks on this type of question because they write at length about one point rather than the several that are asked for. Try to make your answers clear and concise, as space on the examination paper is often limited.

Letts
Q&A

15 THE EARTH AND BEYOND

Question			Answer	Mark
1	(a)		Jupiter is made up of gases.	1
			The Earth is made up of rocks.	1
	(b)	(i)	The very strong magnetic field.	1
		(ii)	Jupiter is further from the Sun than the Earth is. **or**	
			At Jupiter the Sun's gravitational force is weaker.	1
			Its orbital distance is greater	1
			Its orbital speed is less.	1
		(iii)	Jupiter is further from the Sun than the Earth is,	1
			so the intensity of the Sun's radiation is less.	1
	(c)		Io is warmer than the Earth's moon.	1
			Io has an atmosphere. **or** Its surface is changing.	1

> **Examiner's tip** This is an example of a question where you have to interpret the information given in the stem. No marks are awarded for answers such as 'Io is colder than the Earth's moon because it is further from the Sun'.

Question			Answer	Mark
	(d)	(i)	It overheated. **or** It was crushed by the atmospheric pressure. **or**	
			It was destroyed by chemicals.	1
		(ii)	There was a resistive force on the parachute	1
			that reduced its speed.	1
2	(a)		Hydrogen and helium nuclei were forced together at high speeds.	1
			They fused to form the nuclei of heavier elements.	1
	(b)		The Earth is rich in elements that are heavier than hydrogen and helium.	1
			These did not exist when the first stars formed.	1
	(c)		The lighter materials would have moved to the outside of the spinning cloud	1
			leaving the heavier materials on the inside.	1
	(d)		All the objects in the Universe attract each other.	1
			This gravitational force is slowing down the rate of expansion.	1
	(e)		The path of the galaxies can be traced back.	1
			They appear to have started from a common point in space.	1

3   Your completed graph should look like this:

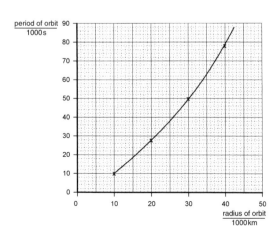

Question	Answer	Mark
	Award marks for:	
	suitable scales and correct labels on the axes,	1
	correct plotting of all the points,	1
	drawing a smooth curve.	1
(b)	The period of orbit increases as the radius of orbit increases.	1

> **Examiner's tip** In answering questions that ask you to identify a trend it is important, when describing the change of one quantity (period of orbit), to specify whether the other quantity (radius of orbit) is increasing or decreasing.

Question	Answer	Mark
(c) (i)	$24 \text{ hours} = 24 \times 60 \times 60 \text{ s} = 86\,400 \text{ s}$	1
	by extrapolating the curve, this gives a radius of 42 000 km	1
(ii)	This orbit is suitable for a communications satellite.	1
	The period is the same as that of the Earth's rotation on its axis OR	
	the satellite always stays above the same point on the Earth's surface.	1

> **Examiner's tip** Communications satellites include those used for satellite television and some telephone links.

Question	Answer	Mark
(d)	The speed decreases with increasing radius of orbit.	1
	When the radius of orbit doubles, the time to complete the orbit is more than double.	1

16 ENERGY RESOURCES AND ENERGY TRANSFER

Question	Answer	Mark
1 (a) (i)	Convection	1
(ii)	Conduction	1
(iii)	Radiation	1
(b) (i)	High energy water molecules transfer energy to plastic molecules,	1
	this causes increased energy of vibration	1
	which is passed on to neighbouring molecules.	1

> **Examiner's tip** A common error made by candidates when describing conduction is to state that heat particles or hot particles travel through the walls. It is important to realise that conduction involves transfer of energy through the vibrations of particles and the interactions with neighbouring particles.

Question	Answer	Mark
(ii)	The outer wall remains cool.	1
2 (a)	Hydroelectric power is renewable; it does not use up any of the Earth's energy resources.	1
	It does not produce carbon dioxide or other greenhouse gases.	1
	It does not leave ash or produce sulphur dioxide.	1

Question	Answer	Mark

(b)   The Sun.   1

(c) (i) Gravitational potential energy in the water   1
changes to kinetic energy as the water falls.   1
This is transferred to electricity in the generators.   1

(ii) change in gpe $= m \times g \times \Delta h$ 1
$= 2.5 \times 10^5 \times 10 \times 190$ 1
$= 4.75 \times 10^8\,\text{J}$ 1

(iii) Max power output $= 60\% \times$ power input   1
$= 0.6 \times 4.75 \times 10^8\,\text{J/s}$ 1
$= 2.85 \times 10^8\,\text{W}$ 1

(iv) Not all the kinetic energy can be removed from the water; it has to have some movement when it leaves the generators.   2

(v) Any two answers from:
pumped storage stations can be brought into operation very rapidly,
they 'use' energy at night when it is readily available,
they do not cause any atmospheric pollution. (1 mark each)   2

3 (a)   Knowledge of formula work = force × distance moved in direction
of force $= Fs$ 1
$= 4000\,\text{N} \times 1.8\,\text{m}$ 1
$= 7200\,\text{J}$ 1

(b)   Work $= 2200\,\text{N} \times 3.6\,\text{m}$ 1
$= 7920\,\text{J}$ 1

(c)   More work has to be done when dragging because of friction forces.   1
The extra energy is transferred to thermal energy.   1
The thermal energy is in the ramp and the load.   1

(d)   The ramp enables a smaller force to be used.   1

4 (a)   kinetic energy $= \frac{1}{2} \times m \times v^2 = \frac{1}{2} \times 80\,\text{kg} \times (12\text{ m/s})^2$ 1
$= 5760\,\text{J}$ 1

Question	Answer	Mark

(b) (i) power = energy transfer ÷ time taken = 5760 J ÷ 8 s   **1**

        = 720 W   **1**

Examiner's tip You must have both the correct answer and unit for the second mark. Note that although a watt is equivalent to a joule/second, J/s is not usually accepted as the unit of power.

(ii) knowledge of formula: energy transfer = force × distance moved   **1**

     force = energy transfer ÷ distance = 5760 J ÷ 48 m   **1**

               = 120 N   **1**

Examiner's tip An alternative approach to answering this question is to calculate the acceleration as -1.5 m/s^2 and then to use F=ma. This would be awarded full marks in an examination.

(iii) ke = $\frac{1}{2} \times m \times v^2 = \frac{1}{2} \times 80\,\text{kg} \times (6\,\text{m/s})^2$ **1**

       = 1440 J   **1**

(iv) There is only one quarter of the energy to be removed from the cycle and cyclist, which is achieved by the force working for one quarter the distance. **1**

17 RADIOACTIVITY

Question	Answer	Mark

1 (a) (i) Any two from:

the air, the ground, rocks, the Sun, waste from nuclear power stations, radiation from testing of nuclear weapons, radioactive materials used in medicine.   1 mark each.   **2**

(ii) Radioactive decay is a random process.   **1**

Examiner's tip The decay of an unstable nucleus cannot be predicted; it could occur at any time, which is why the process of radioactive decay is described as 'random'.

(iii) 1.1 counts/s   **1**

(b) (i) The completed table should show 1.1 counts/s deducted from the count rate to give the corrected count rate:

corrected count rate/counts per s	31.1	28.9	26.6	24.1	21.5	19.8	18.1	16.2	14.8	13.7	12.3	11.0	9.9

   1

(ii) Your completed graph should look like that shown on the next page.

Question	Answer	Mark

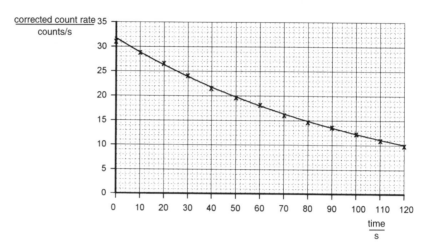

Award marks for:

suitable scales and correct labels on the axes,　　　　　　1

correct plotting of all the points,　　　　　　1

drawing a smooth curve.　　　　　　1

Examiner's tip　Because of the random nature of radioactive decay, all the points cannot be expected to lie precisely on a smooth curve. When drawing the curve, try to balance out the number of points above the curve with the number of points below the curve.

(iii)　Answer in the range 70 to 75 s.　　　　　　1

Explanation to show that more than one pair of readings has been used;

e.g. 74 s to decay from 30 cts/s to 15 cts/s and 71 s to decay from 20 cts/s to 10 cts/s gives an average of 73 s.　　　　　　1

Examiner's tip　Because of the random nature of radioactive decay, the half-life is defined as the average time for half the undecayed nuclei to decay. You need to take more than one measurement from the graph to be able to work out an average.

2　(a)　(i)　They have the same number of protons.　　　　　　1

(ii)　They have different numbers of neutrons.　　　　　　1

Examiner's tip　Isotopes of the same element must have the same number of protons, so the atomic number (the lower number on the left of the symbol) is the same. They have different numbers of neutrons, giving the nuclei different mass numbers (the upper number on the left of the symbol).

(b)　(i)　A beta particle is a high-energy OR fast-moving　　　　　　1

electron.　　　　　　1

(ii)　The nucleus.　　　　　　1

Question	Answer	Mark

A common error is for candidates to state that the beta particle is emitted from the electrons around the nucleus, since the nucleus does not contain any electrons. The emission of a beta particle occurs when a neutron decays into a proton and an electron.

(c) (i) Half-life is the average time — 1

for the number of undecayed nuclei to halve. — 1

(ii) 20 cts/s — 1

A common misunderstanding amongst GCSE candidates is that after two half-lives all the nuclei have decayed. This is not the case; on the average half should decay during one half-life and then half of these (ie one quarter of the original nuclei) during the next half-life and so on.

(iii) One hundred years is a very short time compared to the half-life, — 1

so the rate of decay would show no measurable change. — 1

Radiocarbon dating is suitable for dating objects that are thousands of years old in order that a measurable difference between the activity of the carbon and that of carbon in new objects can be recorded.

18 MOCK EXAMINATION PAPER

Question	Answer	Mark

1 (a) A and F (same number of electrons in outer shell) — 1

(b) A and C or D and F (same number of shells) — 1

(c) B — 1

(d) 1 — 1

(e) D and E (Both metals) — 2

(f) (i) One mark each. — 2

(ii) D reacts with A – ionic bonding. C reacts with F – covalent bonding. — 2

This question involves an understanding of electron arrangements, and bonding. Candidates are often confused with the two types of bonding – ionic and covalent.

2 (a) $Zn + 2HCl \rightarrow ZnCl_2 + H_2$ — 2
One mark for correct formula and one mark for correct balancing.

(b) (i) 2, 4 and 5. All three correct, none incorrect – 2 marks. — 2
Award 1 mark if two correct, even if one is incorrect.

Question	Answer	Mark
(ii)	The same mass of zinc is used in each experiment.	1
(iii)	Catalyst Copper is produced $CuSO_4 + Zn \rightarrow ZnSO_4 + Cu$ Copper is the catalyst, not copper sulphate.	4
(iv)	Magnesium	1

Examiner's tip This question is testing your understanding of rates of reaction and reactivity series of metals. It is clearly about rates of reaction but to score full marks in (b)(iii) you need to understand displacement reactions.

3	(a)	(i)	Correct plotting. Deduct 1 mark for an incorrect plot.	2

(ii)	A curve through the points.	1
(b)	With increasing temperature the solubility increases.	1
	The rate of increase increases with temperature, i.e. it is not proportional.	1
(c)	83.5 g at 80°C and 16 g at 20° C 67.5 g	2
(d)	X – unsaturated.	1
	Y – saturated.	1
	Z – unsaturated.	1

4	(a)	Very low concentration of carbon dioxide.	0.5
		Carbon dioxide used up during photosynthesis.	1
	(b)	Concentration similar to the air.	0.5
		Balance between carbon dioxide used up by photosynthesis and carbon dioxide produced when snails respire.	1
	(c)	High.	0.5
		Photosynthesis cannot take place but plant respires.	1
	(d)	Very high.	0.5
		Plant and snails respire.	1
		Round up any half marks to the nearest whole number at the end.	

Examiner's tip It is important that you use the words photosynthesis and respiration in your answers.

Question	Answer	Mark
5 (a)	Transport semen rather than live bulls.	1
	Use artificial insemination.	1
(b)	Meiosis	1
	Mitosis	1
(c) (i)	Bb	1
(ii)	BB Bb Bb bb All correct 2 marks, 3 correct 1 mark.	2
	Some form of correct genetic diagram.	1
(d)	Pick hornless male and female animals.	
	Allow them to mate.	
	Select best of the offspring.	
	Repeat the process several times.	
	Process is called selective breeding.	
	Any three points	3

Examiner's tip   It is important to spell meiosis and mitosis correctly. Often an answer given is miosis. By adding just one letter this could be either term.
Do not confuse selective breeding with genetic engineering.

6 (a) (i)	It increases.	1
(ii)	It decreases.	1

Examiner's tip   Resistance is a measure of the opposition to electrical current, so the greater the resistance, the less current passes for a given voltage.

(b)	voltage = current × resistance	1
	= 5 A × 24 Ω	1
	= 120 V	1

Examiner's tip   Always use these steps in doing calculations: *formula, substitute values, answer* and *unit*. Note that you would not be awarded the last mark if your answer had no unit or the wrong unit.

(c)	Infra-red and light. (1 mark each.)	2

7 (a) (i)	average speed = distance travelled ÷ time taken	1
	= 162.5 m ÷ 25 s	1
	= 6.5 m/s	1
(ii)	Sometimes the cyclist would be travelling faster and sometimes slower.	1
(b)	acceleration = increase in speed ÷ time taken	1
	= (6 m/s–3 m/s) ÷ 5 s	1
	= 0.6 m/s^2	1
(c) (i)	force = mass × acceleration	1
	= 85 kg × 0.6 m/s^2	1
	= 51 N	1

Answers to mock examination paper

Question	Answer	Mark

Examiner's tip This question shows how important it is that you learn the formulae on page 6. A calculation of speed or an acceleration is often worth three marks.

(ii)	Resistive forces act on the cycle.	1
	These resistive forces act in the backwards direction.	1

Examiner's tip The unbalanced force is the difference between the forwards force and the sum of the backwards forces.

---

8 (a) Award one mark for each correct change in direction.

2

Examiner's tip Total internal reflection occurs in the prism because the angle of incidence is greater than the critical angle.

(b)	(i)	Refraction	1
	(ii)	It is decreased.	1
	(iii)	There is no effect.	1

Examiner's tip Only the speed and wavelength change when light is refracted: the frequency always stays the same.

9			
	(i)	Convection	1
	(ii)	Conduction	1
	(iii)	Radiation	1
	(iv)	Evaporation	1

Examiner's tip Evaporation of the water from the swimmer's body causes cooling as the water takes energy away from the skin. The same mechanism cools us when we sweat.

Marking your test

Use the marking scheme to mark your test. If you are not sure about any of your answers, ask your teacher. When you have a mark for the test out of 75 marks you can use this table to estimate your likely grade. Remember, however, that this is just one test which tests only part of the syllabus and so you cannot be sure you will get this grade every time. It will give you an indication of your level of achievement.

Mark in the test	Grade
Over 68	A*
60–67	A
49–59	B
38–48	C
26–37	D
Less than 25	Ungraded

Letts

Q&A